We Are Only Visiting

We Are Only Visiting

THE ART AND WRITING OF
KATHRYN ELIZABETH CARTER

Edited by Helen Carter

To Kathryn, never without you.

Carter Family

Contents

Speeches 113

Introduction

It seems life is better if you just live it ...
It seems to me that we should live each day as it comes.
Kathryn Carter, 1983–2003

This book chronicles the writing journey of a talented girl. In just twenty years Kathryn Elizabeth Carter packed in so many experiences. She made lasting friendships, she played, she was imaginative, she studied, she travelled, she painted, she performed, she debated, she ran fast, she fell in love and she endeared herself to many.

Kathryn Elizabeth, known to most of her friends as Kat, loved to write from an early age. Her first forays were stories and poems filled with spelling mistakes and quirky ideas, most stimulated by talented teachers at primary (Dobroyd Point Primary School, Haberfield) and secondary school (Presbyterian Ladies' College (PLC), Sydney). And friends, like Hayley, who played imaginative and adventurous games with Kat in the garden or Stella with whom she could have deep discussions about life, language and art, for hours. Friends and friendship were always an important part of Kathryn's life.

Then in Year 7 she was asked to enter a public speaking competition, Rostrum Voice of Youth. She not only won the first round, but she was excited to find people her age who were just as interested in words as she was. Rostrum was the start of her interest in public speaking. Encouraged by her speech teacher, Ms Bennetts at PLC, Kathryn flourished as a writer and speaker. She enjoyed the limelight but also the company and she went on to enter other competitions such as the Independent Girls' Schools Association (IGSA) competitions, the SMH Plain Speaking competition, and internal school competitions. Kathryn also continued with Rostrum competitions throughout her high school years and kept in touch with Rostrum and many of her former competitors after she left school.

Her speeches reflect her time, the nineties, when the mobile phone was just beginning to influence people and the Olympics was on everyone's mind.

Drama and creative writing were still very much of interest. In Year 7 she won a PLC internal school creative writing competition, the youngest to ever do so. And, five years later, her major work for English in the HSC was a play. Kathryn was also a keen debater, enjoying the power of persuasion.

From primary school onwards, she loved to be on a stage, performing in productions like *William Tell* and *Joseph and His Amazing Technicolour Dream Coat* in primary school and *The Dresser* at Trinity in Year 9 and lead parts in *Godspell* and *Guys and Dolls* in Years 10

and 11. She made wonderful friendships and many of those friends still keep in touch with her family.

She also entered eisteddfods, especially the Inner West Eisteddfod, encouraged by her friend Jenna. They would do monologues and duologues from Shakespeare. They were often very successful, but it was the experience of performing that they really enjoyed. And she was proud of the growing number of pockets of achievement on her blazer. Kat and Jenna were also on an episode of Squawk TV after Kathryn wrote a suggestion about exploring the recycling of fashion.

In 2001 Kathryn was awarded the first Australian Speech Communication Association (ASCA) prize for speech and drama.

On leaving school she started her own business, Cheshire Drama, where she coached and taught speech and drama. And at the University of Sydney she continued her interest in drama. This time she worked behind the scenes as a director of *Equus* and *Dangerous Liaisons* and she began a social group called High Society.

Kathryn was posthumously awarded her BA from the University of Sydney.

Each year Kathryn's love of drama and public speaking is remembered and passed on to encourage other young people, with prizes given in her name: for drama at PLC Sydney, for Rostrum's junior winner of the state final, for a Shakespearean performance piece at the Inner West Eisteddfod and for art history at the University of Sydney.

Kathryn was lucky to have travelled around the world with her parents from a young age. She went to kindergarten in Oxford, England, and fourth class in Atlanta, Georgia, USA. She enjoyed being a part of the *Journal of Contract Law* conferences. She wanted to help and enjoyed the adult company. At 18 years old she travelled on her own to England and then around Europe with a friend.

Kathryn had only twenty years on this earth but in that time she touched many lives. Most remember her smile. And her pure joy at living. You may have caught that smile in the Banana advertisement 'na na na na make your body sing'. Her parents remember the daughter who shared their love of Beatles and Dr Who, who was frightened of slippery dips, who played *Upwords* in the garden each weekend, who danced and sang and laughed, who hated the day to end and refused to ever say goodbye, who cried as she left Disneyland because she didn't want the experience to end, who loved visiting her grandparents whose wisdom she valued, who taught Sunday School with her mum and who loved and appreciated that her aunty Margaret always came to hear her speak.

Although she made everyone feel special, she particularly loved her friends and her family and relished their company. She would be delighted and grateful that so many of her friends keep in contact with her parents (as indeed her parents are). We know they still miss her.

This book is for you, to laugh, to cry, to remember.

And if you didn't know her this might give you some insight into a young soul who lived every moment to the fullest.

Presciently, when she was 17 years old, Kathryn wrote and gave a speech 'We Are Only Visiting' (page 162) in which she said: 'I believe that we should embrace the fact we are only visiting and take hold of every opportunity … we should not only enjoy what we have, while we have it, but also look forward to the next place we are going'. Kathryn lived her words and remains an inspiration to all who knew and loved her.

Acknowledgements

There are many people to thank who encouraged and stimulated Kathryn's endeavours. Her Dobroyd Point primary school teachers Ms Eyres, Ms Simons, Mr Readett and Ms Contos. Her stimulating teachers in English, art and drama at PLC, particularly Ms Bennetts and Ms Coleman. Aunty Margaret who never missed a speaking competition.

And the many people who encouraged and helped us bring this book to fruition. We cannot mention everyone but we would like particularly to thank Therese Bennetts, Rostrum Voice of Youth, ASCA and PLC Sydney.

After the basic manuscript was located and selected Rosemary Peers and Diana Murray converted the disparate components into this truly beautiful work. We thank them both for their excellent suggestions and work.

We also wish to acknowledge some of the inspirations behind Kathryn's writing: William Shakespeare, Robert Fulgham, The Beatles, Buffy the Vampire Slayer, Dr Who, Mary Poppins, Enid Blyton's *The Wishing Chair*. Thank you also to those who gave permission for their comments and photos to be used in this publication.

We are sure that reading Kathryn's work will bring a smile to your face, but perhaps also a wistful sigh as to what might have been.

Helen and John Carter
Sydney, October 2021

POEMS

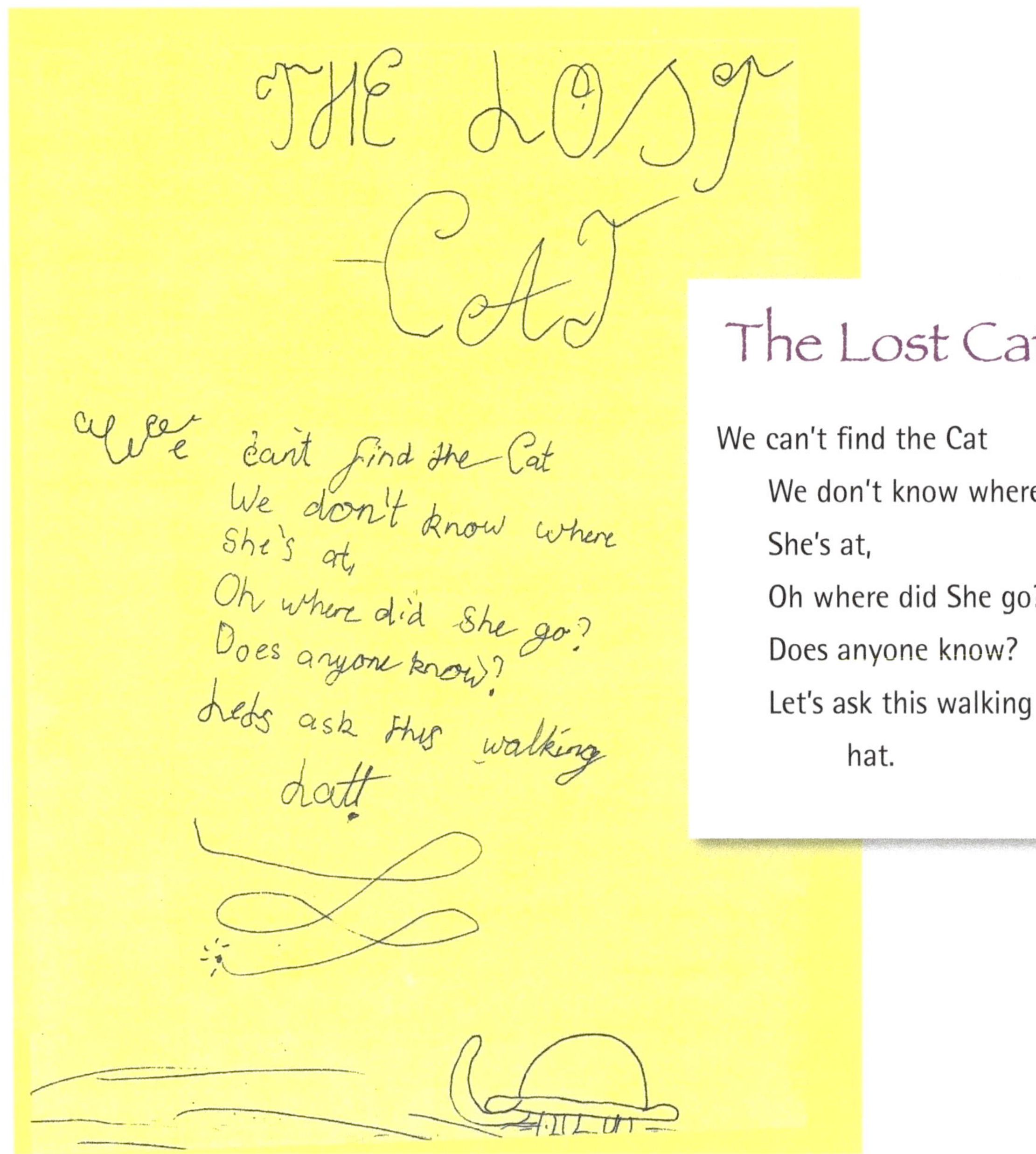

The Lost Cat

We can't find the Cat

We don't know where

She's at,

Oh where did She go?

Does anyone know?

Let's ask this walking

hat.

What the Frog Said

When the Frog from under the canopy
Said *hello* to Penelope
She did not run and hide.
She simply replied
'ISN'T IT A LOVELY DAY!'

When the snake turned to a Hen
Faithful old Pen shook her head
Then plainly said
"ISN'T IT A LOVELY DAY!"

But when the world started to fight
And Penelope lost her sight,
She picked up her gun,
And started to run,
It was no longer a Lovely day!

Ode to Ties

Winter,
time for fun,
Lots of things can be
done, But, oh me oh my,
it's time for the Dreaded
TIE!
How are we
supposed to have
fun? When we're busy
being Hung? Tied in a knot,
It's really hot, Always getting
left behind, And it's always
hard to find! Choking,
slowly most unpleasant,
Would YOU want one
for a present? So
when you're hot or
tied in a knot.
Think of us,
Tied up and
boiling
hot!

Published in the PLC
College Crow magazine,
September 1995

That's My Australia

Kookabarra laughs from the wattle tree, Koala munches in the gumtrees.

Kangaroo hops around, onto the road, dodges the cars.

Hoping* around surrounded by people.

Talking and walking around.

Sky Skrapers scrape the sky.

Toorists taking photos.

Back to the bush as the Aussie sun sets, all its colours etched vibrantly on the water.

While the Kookabarra, the Koala, and the Kangaroo sleep softly and the bats and the possums come out.

   That's my

   Australia

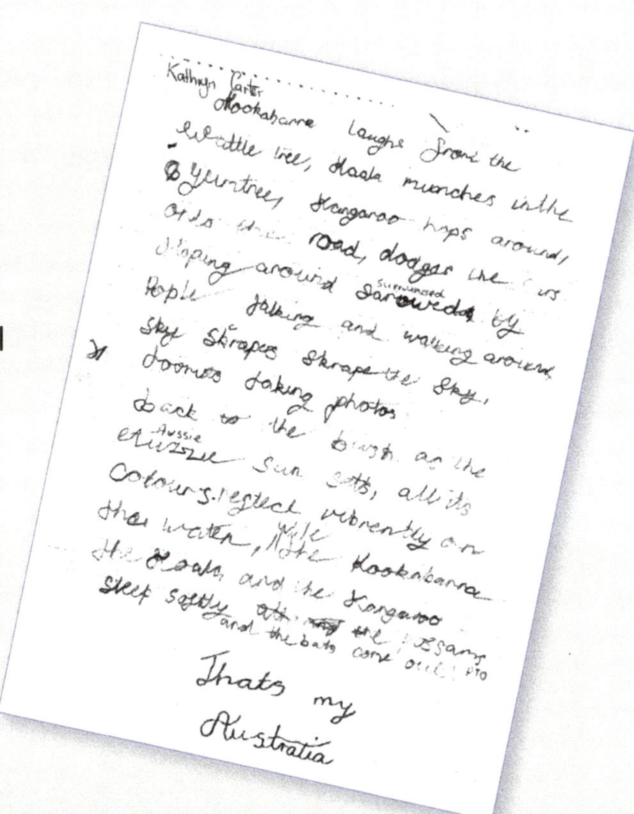

Terrific Teddies

Terrific Teddies never too many!

Everyone extremely cute.

Daring, death defying diving down from the shelf.

Dad, can I get some more Teddies?

Yes is what I want to hear!

But I have a lot.

Even still you can't have enough Teddies!

And I love them all!

Really good company!

Special friends!

Roller Coasters

Here we are finally
    The queue took hours,
        But now I'm here
            Oh dear,
                The tummy turns,
                The front is supposed to be good,
            I wonder if I should,
        Swap with the people behind me?
Slowly at first,
    Up, Up, Up and Up
        Will it ever stop going up and up and up!
            Down round over and under,
                What a wonder,
                    The feeling,
                Terrific, no terrible in between,
            I shut my eyes so what's to come cannot be seen!
            Round and round people gasp,
        Will it ever end?
        Another bend, my stomach back there somewhere!
    Over,
under,
    jolt,
        then stop,
            back under over,
                round,
                    my stomach is still on the ground!
                    In the tunnel dark,
                something jumps out,
            I hate the dark!
        Down with a drop suddenly.
My stomach is definitely not with me!
        BANG,
                STOP this is the end!
        I know something for sure
            NOT AGAIN!

Onomatopoeia

Snotty, Slimy, Tissues
Stick in your pockets,
They Slither and Squelch,
Shrivel and Smell,
Shed and Crumble
And are Absolutely revolting!

Alliteration

Kitty cats catch coffee caramels,
Continuously,
Carefully caring for each one of
them.
The Kitty cats carry them cautiously,
To the coffee cabinet
where carrots are also kept.

An Easter Dream

Ones a pon a time.

When every one in the world could see the Easter chick (not the Easter Buny.)

Lots of things hapond.

Like dragons steling prinsesers and piinsers saviling them.

The Sea

*Cool, smooth, gentle, soft, ripple, the waves are
cool and peaceful, back and forth they glide. Splish
splash, sssssssssshhhhhhhh, they laze slowly across
the sand and back again, catching sea weed, bark
and shells, and rippling, steeling them back to the
sea.*
SPLASH
SPLAT
SPLOT
HIGH
DIVE
It hits the water with a great KA,SPLAT!
KA,SMASH
PLASH
CRASH
CLASH
KA,PASH

*Smooth, relaxed, gentle, peaceful, cool, spills,
calm, dancing in the sun.
Bopping, swaying, welcoming,
The sea is perfect!
AND THEN.......*

For Grandma

Kindness that Produced Warmth.
A Warmth that brought Happiness.
As the Blue Bells play their Serenade across Scotland,
She will be remembered.
A gentle Smile,
A soothing hand.
A comforting presence,
Someone everyone knew,
She will be missed.
Always smiling,
Always caring.
A Mother, a Grandmother with a sense of humour,
She always has and always will be Loved.

Kathryn wrote this for her grandma's funeral in October 1997 and it was included in the order of service.

Little Jack Horner?

Alpha: Little Jack Horner, sat in a corner

Beta: Eating a Christmas pie...

Alpha: Great way to spend Christmas.

Beta: All alone.

Alpha: He put in his thumb

Beta: And he pulled out a plumb

Alpha: But just because it rhymes, it doesn't make it any better.

Beta: Even if it rhymed twice.

The Surrealist Painter

Walked down the street,
The sun shone brightly, burning, blazing hot.
The street lights danced in the darkness adding a
Dim light to the surroundings. The sundial struck midnight.
I reached my studio and headed straight to the garden.

I felt safe in the confinement, some may have felt
Claustrophobic with the six walls.
My canvas in front of me, I began to paint the
Daylight—landscape of the stars that danced like
Fairies above my head.
I stared at the far horizon.
My brush swiped across the canvas, in messy
Serenading strokes—ever so delicate.
My hand wobbled and slipped, the painting was ruined.
I cursed my brush.
My head whirled round like a lounge chair.
It was getting late, the morning was nearly over, so
In a mournful despair I retired to my bed.
The oak trees that surrounded me swayed and
Danced, their faces wrinkled and worried, their
Leaves creased as they got older-wiser.
My garden was bare and dry,
The water from the nearby lake flooded by.

The flowers danced in their plain, bright, dazzling
Colours as a friendly giraffe pranced by
The willow tree women danced around my bed.
They sang to the sky, their straight, radiating hair
drooped over my bed,
Drawers and doors opened at their feet and
Cupboards at their chests.
The man with two dimensions to his face
Cheerfully wallowed in.
People have spent hours looking at his worried and cheerful face.
That was when I could paint and the world was at my feet,
Galleries paid me a lot.
Soon my world will fade,
The willow tree women, the two-sided man,
The starry, sunny skies will be no more.
Just the dream of a crazy man,
Just the madness of his soul.
Just the fantasy of a boring life.
Just the thought that stuck in your head.
Just the anxiety that had to escape.
Just the dream you never forgot.
Merely a message hidden too deep
Just a story that had to be told.
Just a message that was misunderstood.
Just a memory, just a memory.

1997-98

One for My Baby and One More for…

It takes some arrogance to admit, that
Though I have walked only eighteen years I
Have inspired poetry and music
All by the flick of my hair, by my smile
(Which is not my own) and lips a siren
Red (painted of course), and eyes that sparkle,
(Although not a single one has considered
How and why they come to shine.)
Such is my life, and such is my world.

I have been called 'muse' by many a tongue. Which,
Is sweet to hear, but hard to comprehend
And for some unexplainable reason
Conjures up feelings of bitter resentment,
As though I control something that should not
Be controlled, and in such a state I lose my identity.
So I sit and I ponder with carefully
Placed untidy hair, and an out-fit that
Suits my mood, and I wonder why and how

And what I have done to deserve such a
Double-edged sword of flattery and fate, what
I did to cause such beauty. Many a
Gallant and profound reason could be sung
But I do not believe any of them and
While I love my curse, and could not live without
It, I hate the very essence of it.
I do not trust its origins. A world
Like mine is one that can be loved only with
Pain. An identity only for others to capture.

And yet, for you, I would exist only to inspire.
To inspire anything by you is
To live a thousand years and to love every
Second. I have heard tales of women who sit
By their lover's side hour by hour and hold pencils.
I always thought it was a ridiculous
activity, that would inspire nothing
but boredom, but by you I would sit for ever and never
grow tired.

There Is Nothing Left to Say

There is nothing to say. Nothing to write.
No words that can capture, no phrase that can
Wrap such anguish, such pain, such perfection
Into one neat, tidy and well-placed construction.
A smile is painted.
I could tell you many a tale, and
I probably will. What good does that do?

A sip to save a soul. An hour to
Waste. Seconds disappear as each moment
Passes from glass to taste to memory.
It is lost. It is gone. Or so it seems.

Free from point or purpose it has left.
It leaves nothing but ice and emptiness.
Gone because avoidance is turning into
Addiction. Gone because the light has gone

From the world. My world is dark and I am
Afraid. I fear I have lost the sun. I
Am hollow and the pathetic shell that
Has survived this ordeal aches and quivers
And regrets ever even shading from the
Light.

2001

Write Me a Letter

Write me a letter where we can be together

Write purpose into postage and seal with intention

Write me a letter from an ever reaching river

Write so that sentiment sets sail.

Write me a letter under an unpredictable moon

Write me the stars and gaze at the page

Write me a letter fast pace on a train

Write in the fraction of a moment of silence

and fill it with written words

Write me a letter from the bottom of a glass.

Write as dinner is served.

Savour the page and order the words

Write me a letter in which words will not suffice.

Write yourself into an envelope so that

I can study you last thing at night

PLAYS AND MONOLOGUES

When I'm 64

Have you seen those young boys with their long hair? Disgusting it is! My friend May doesn't agree with me, you know what she said, She said 'Didn't Jesus have long hair?' 'Well' I said 'at least his was clean'. People say those Liverpool boys are very clean but I don't know. All that wigglin' around just isn't proper! I don't know what the world is coming to! Girls screamin' and shoutin' 'Paul, George, John, Ringo!' *Ringo* honestly I doubt it's even his real name. I doubt it's anyone's real name. I doubt it's even a name! I mean what's wrong with somethin' like Peter, at least that's a real name, and a sensible one too. I heard they've all taken drugs, not Penicillin mind you, *ma r i juana*! Now I hardly think that's a good example for our children do you? Oh, where are my fags?

The songs they sing these days. I heard that one of them had a hidden message, a code like for drugs! *Lucy in the Sky with Diamonds*. Sounds harmless enough but it really means LSD. That's a drug you know. I mean should our children be listenin' to these sorts of things. I mean what happened to Frank Sinatra? Now he has a sensible name and he sings sensible songs, good clean songs. I don't know what's happening to the world. It seems the good old Waltz has completely vanished for our younguns. Look at the dances they've got these days, Sheila tells me I'm not IN, but I tell her I'm always in if she'd ever come over for tea. The skirts the girls these days wear! If they were any shorter they'd be belts! And the blouses; show everythin' they do! I tell my daughter, Sandra, that if she wears things like that she leaves no mystery, but she doesn't seem to care.

I like trains, don't you? Sandra told me I should catch a plane. All up there in the sky, no thank you! Gives me the shivers just thinkin' about it. So I told her I was only goin' to Manchester and those plane tickets are expensive! Cost an arm and a leg just to go somewhere you can get to by train. Just silly if you ask me.

It's my cousin's wedding. Apparently she's lost a lot of weight for it. Well I said it's about time. Always been a tubby thing she has, I was surprised she found anyone at all. Still, she is a lovely person and as that song goes that my daughter's always playin'; *All you need is Love*. By the Bugs or someone that is. I asked Sandra if she was goin' to their concert. I said 'You goin' to see the Bugs?' Well she just shook her head and said I wasn't with it.

With what I'll never know.

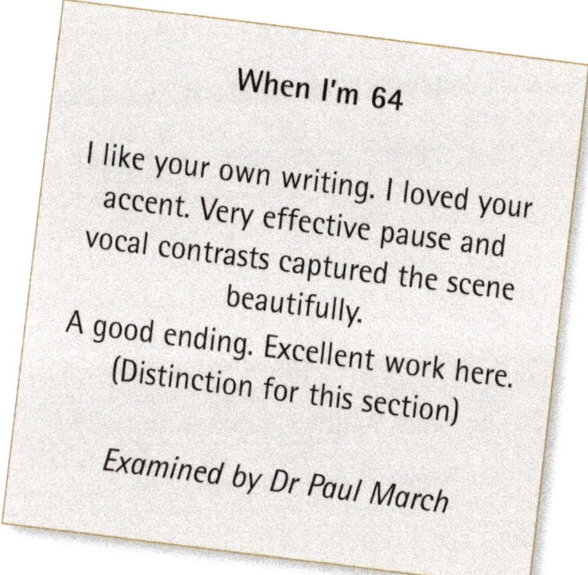

When I'm 64

I like your own writing. I loved your accent. Very effective pause and vocal contrasts captured the scene beautifully.
A good ending. Excellent work here.
(Distinction for this section)

Examined by Dr Paul March

There Is Nothing Like Company

There are people who are old,
Don't leave them out in the cold,
Send them to us,
Pack them up in the bus.
Send us your money,
We don't care if they've gone a bit funny,
And when they expire,
We will meet every desire.
A funeral we will provide,
We are especially good with people who have died.
Roses will be sent,
And with your consent.
We will cremate or bury.
The funeral will be happy and merry!
There is nothing like life.
And we savour it through all strife,
Big sitting rooms are supplied,
There is no place to run and hide.

Meals are included in the price,

We have a cat to keep away mice.

We go on outings every Thursday,

So don't delay.

Old people won't last for ever,

NO matter how clever.

We aren't far from the city. It would be a pity

For an old person to die alone.

So they can come here and moan,

There is nothing like company.

Grandad

In the late morning, nearly lunchtime, an old but strong figure walked down to the bus stop, sat himself down and started to absorb the sunshine. Positioned next to him was a similarly old and lonely person. The strong figure began to talk in a thick Somerset accent.

'Hello. Been listening to the cricket? Oh, they've really let the side down! The English are playin' terribly! Almost makes ya' ashamed to be an Englishman! I've been unlucky today with the horses, First, Third and Fourth would 'ave paid Six Hundred Dollars! Do you ever bet on the horses? Two, Four and Six in the Fifth race. Number Two will come up on the outside and surprise 'em all. You'll see! Oh. I'd really like a beer, nothin' like a bit of sun and a cool beer! I love the sun, that's why we moved out to Australia, that and my job—I was a printer you know, one of the best! I polished this um, oh, forget what it's called. Anyway I polished it so well it's in a museum! Still there it is! We also moved out 'cos there's more here for the children. My youngest son, he has just been made a Professor and his daughter has just won some competition for arguin' or somethin'. We're all very proud; in the paper she was! She's just got braces—poor thing. They don't look too bad— eighteen months she has to 'ave 'em in! Costin' a fortune—I don't see what for, somethin' about a bite. My youngest daughter's children had 'em too, but they got them off 'cos they hurt too much!

'I remember when I got these false things. I was lyin' on my bed when this man walked in with this mask, he put it over my mouth but I were never unconscious! There were blood and teeth everywhere, on the ceiling, the carpet even the curtains! Wife has trouble with her teeth, keep fallin' out! She has the longest toenails you know. She kicks me in bed, she hits me and all—she doesn't half thrash about! Still, got-a-love 'er

'Saw this movie last night on the **S.B.S.** Amazin' it was! It were called *Wolfman* or something. About this man who ate a rotten hot dog and turned into a wolf at midnight!

Amazin' photography! This woman—his girlfriend who was also a reporter wanted to see for herself. It were terrifyin'! I was scared stiff! All this hair grew out of his cheeks—I was frozen, then from out of the top of his head popped two ears, amazin'! I don't know how they do it! Things they do these days. If you ever see it advertised, I would watch it if I were you—you'll never see anythin' like it!'

As a blue bus pulls up, the stunned, silent man gets up to go. The pair exchange farewell nods and the silent being steps onto the bus taking the thoughts of The Cricket, Horse racing, Teeth, the stranger's family and movies from the S.B.S. with him.
An old lady sits down next to the old man still absorbing the sun.

'Hello. Been listening to the cricket? Oh, they've really let the side down! The English are playin' terribly! ...'

Infinite Darkness

Duologue *(two girls in a small rowboat,*
in the dreams of a lonely child)

Cecelia: It's a bit dark.

Amelia: Scared are we?

Cecelia: No. Are you?

Amelia: No, of course not ... are you?

Cecelia: You already asked me that.

Amelia: Oh, yeah.

Cecelia: It's a funny thing isn't it.

Amelia: What?

Cecelia: The dark.

Amelia: Cold, icy, suspicious ... no I can't say I can
see anything humorous about it.

Cecelia: Of course you can't ... its too dark to see anything.

Amelia: I was speaking metaphorically.

Cecelia: Well it serves you right then doesn't it.

Amelia: What?

Cecelia: What?

Amelia: What?

Cecelia: What?

Amelia: What were we talking about again?

Cecelia: I don't know. I wonder what's over there.

Kathryn and
Hayley, friends
since kindergarten

Amelia: Infinite darkness no doubt.

Cecelia: Really? How interesting. I wonder what it looks like.

Amelia: Quite dark I imagine.

Cecelia: But how do you know? How does anybody know? Has anybody ever been into infinite
           darkness, had a look around and then come out and said 'boy it's dark in there'?

Amelia: You definitely have too many thoughts.

Cecelia: I wonder what they look like.

Amelia: What?

Cecelia: Thoughts.

Amelia: I don't think they look like anything.

Cecelia: But how do you know? How does anybody know? Has anybody ever been ...

Amelia: Please don't start that again.

Cecelia: Oh. Why are we here?

Amelia: Because I have a note.

Cecelia: What kind of note?

Amelia: An important one.

Cecelia: Wow! Can I see it?

Amelia: No.

Cecelia: Why? Please ... it's not everyday I see something important.

Amelia: You are a very sad person you know.

Cecelia: No I'm not.

Amelia: Yes, yes you are. In fact, if there was a competition for the most sadly pathetic person
           you would probably win. Even if the grand duke and duchess of the great land of sad
           and pathetic people entered, bribed all the judges and did something particularly sad
           just for the hell of it. Even in this extreme situation—you would probably still win.

Cecelia: That wasn't very nice. Besides, I've never heard of the duke and duchess of the sadly pathetic people.

Amelia: Of course you haven't. I just made them up.

Cecelia: Well then it wasn't a very well thought out insult if none of the people in the insult actually exist.

Amelia: Just shut up.

Cecelia: Now you are getting defensive.

Amelia: No I'm not.

Cecelia: Yes you are.

Amelia: No I'm not.

Cecelia: Yes you are.

Amelia: No I'm not.

Cecelia: Yes you are.

Amelia: No I'm not.

Cecelia: Yes you ... what were we arguing about again?

Amelia: I was hoping you knew that.

Cecelia: No, I lost the plot a long time ago.

Amelia: I noticed.

Cecelia: So what's in this note?

Amelia: Something important.

Cecelia: What?

Amelia: I don't know.

Cecelia: Where are we taking it then?

Amelia: In that direction. As far as our trusty little boat will take us.

Hayley and Kat

Cecelia: I don't like water.

Amelia: Why?

Cecelia: It's too wet.

Amelia: This is going to be a very, very long trip.

Cecelia: Oh, I hope not. Oh, well, never mind if it is. We can amuse ourselves. How are you at charades? I used to be fantastic. When I was little, well actually about 8 years ago was the last time we played ... (*does a few calculations on her fingers*)—so I must have been six. Well, anyway ... we used to play every Thursday night, and I used to win every time—but then everyone else started getting better than me ... Shall we play now? (*She stands up excited and the pair sway violently side to side as if the boat was about to sink.*)

Amelia: Sit down before you get us both drowned.

Cecelia: How about eye spy then. It's a safe game.

Amelia: Please go away.

Cecelia: I can't! We're on a boat silly.

Amelia: How could I forget.

Cecelia: I don't know.

Amelia: What?

Cecelia: How you could forget we're on a boat. I don't know about you but I am mighty uncomfortable.

Amelia: I think I can see lights!

Cecelia: So can I!

Amelia: I think we must be there!

Cecelia: Where?

Amelia: Where we are taking the note.

Cecelia: I wonder what it's like?

Amelia: Where?

Cecelia: There.

Amelia: A lot like home I imagine.

Cecelia: But how do you know? How does anyone know. Has anybody ever been there, had a look around and come back and said 'boy it's just like home there'?

Amelia: I thought I told you to stop that.

Cecelia: Sorry. Actually, it does look a lot like home.

Amelia: A very lot like home.

Cecelia: A very, very lot like home.

Amelia: A very, very, very, lot like home.

Cecelia: You know what I think.

Amelia: Very rarely, thank God.

Cecelia: I think it is home.

Amelia: All evidence would point us in that direction.

Cecelia: And so would the wind it seems. So, what does the note say?

Amelia: I don't know. No ... I have been told not to open it ... I promised ... No ... Don't give me that look ... Oh ... stop it ... I gave my word ... oh, alright ... Let me see... (*unfolding the piece of paper she had been holding*) ... it's blank.

Cecelia: How odd.

Amelia: Maybe ...

Cecelia: Maybe what?

Amelia: Maybe they were trying to get rid of us.

Cecelia: Why would they want to do that?

Amelia: I have no idea. You're right, it's a silly thought really.

* * *

One Rhyme or Two

Alpha: A wise man once said: 'The owl and the pussy cat went to sea in a beautiful pea-green boat.'

Beta: The truth is that the boat wasn't green at all.

Alpha: No one knows what colour it actually was, but it really wasn't green.

Beta: The fact is the pair were not in love at all.

Alpha: That is why the boat wasn't green.

Beta: You see, they were both very lonely.

Alpha: Very lonely.

Beta: Very very lonely.

Alpha: Very lonely indeed.

Beta: In fact no one missed them at all, even though they sailed away for a year and a day.

Alpha: I mean nothing more needs to be said—considering their destination was a land where the bong trees grow— complete with its own talking pig.

Beta: Loneliness can do terrible things to you.

Alpha: Very terrible things.

Beta: Very, very terrible things.

Alpha: Very terrible things indeed.

Beta: In fact as far as 'things' go, loneliness can do the worst.

2000

No Sugar, Two Lumps

Character List

MASTER OF CEREMONIES: The Master of Ceremonies is the 'Ringleader' of the play. He is a neutral character, but is revealed to be male at the end of the play. However, this is not of great importance. He takes on an authoritative role and tells the story of the play. He is a very 'straight' and almost patronising character, except in the opening monologue where he is quite cheeky, charming and Hamlet-like. He speaks quite casually *with* the audience rather than *to* the audience. He is very 'well pronounced' throughout the play, until the end where he slips into a cockney accent. His whole manner at this point in the play should be a stark contrast to his refined, constrained and formal mannerisms used in the majority of the play. He is nothing more than a persona throughout the play, until the very end where his authority is upturned.

'THE FOUR OLD WOMEN'

To be played by four men dressed in drag as old women. They are two-dimensional, gossiping stereotypes. They are written to be performed in an English Liverpool accent, however, they can be played as stereotypical old women from any nation. They are highly comic characters and are 'larger than life'. They are characters or rather stereotypes that everyone should be familiar with.

MRS THRATCHET

She is in her late 30s to early 40s. She is old enough to be a mother of several children, but not a grandmother. She has been treated badly by men and in *Time Is of the Essence* she is quite bitter and cynical. She smokes, is hard, cold and abrupt. She is not meant to be likeable, in fact the aim is that she confronts the audience, and they are forced to judge her negatively. She is medium in height and in build—she has quite an attractive figure. She is dressed in cheap clothes that once were bright but have been washed so many times that they have faded. In *A Huff and a Puff* she is younger and her mannerisms contrast with those in *Time Is of the Essence*. In this scene MRS THRATCHET is the picture of virgin pureness. She is timid, shy and bashful. At this point in time she is married to MR THRATCHET, but has not been for very long. In the last scene, MRS THRATCHET abandons all the extreme characteristics of the other two scenes. Instead she is quite normal and caring, just stressed.

Characters in *Domestic Life*

FLY: Is played by TOMMY THRATCHET. He has a very low self-esteem, is quite intelligent but verges on neurotic. He is lonely and desperate for friends and attention. He feels quite sorry for himself, but is not completely sure why. He knows he is lonely, but almost blames himself for it. He is a small boy, quite 'stocky' and short, with dark hair.

CAT: Is played by SALLY THRATCHET. In this scene she is a stereotypical cat and therefore uses typical cat-like movements and a cat-like manner of speaking. She is seductive, self-absorbed and stupid. A sleek bimbo. She is tall and thin. She is not at all 'curvy' but rather straight up and down. Something that SALLY THRATCHET is quite disappointed about.

MR THRATCHET

In *As Time Goes By* MR THRATCHET regrets losing his wife. His pride has been hurt and he has a pessimistic and hopeless attitude. He feels very sorry for himself and at the same time blames himself. However, he blames himself in a way that suggests he feels that there was actually nothing he could have done about it because he is so foolish and the world in general hates him. He is weak and appears to be talking to himself. He is quite a short man with a stocky build. He wears a brown suit, which is old and has always been out of fashion. In *A Huff and a Puff* he is just a very two-dimensional, walk-on character. He appears to be submissive, but only with the aim of making MR WOLF look good. In the last scene he shows that he is not as weak as he appeared, instead he is also quite a normal, everyday man.

Characters in *The 69th Floor*

GIRL is played by SALLY THRATCHET. In this scene she is a flirt. She giggles, and will do anything to get out of the apartment. She plays along with the Window Washer in an exaggerated manner that is reminiscent of any pre-conceived ideas about girls with blonde hair. However, she has mousy brown hair, and is dressed in very tight clothes, which do not so much make her more attractive, but rather emphasise her straight and curveless figure.

WINDOW WASHER is played by MR WOLF. In this scene he must be dressed in plain overalls with an old blue shirt underneath and a lot of padding or even a 'fat-suit'. It is essential that he looks very different in this scene compared to how he looks in *A Huff and a Puff*, to the degree where he is almost unrecognisable. He plays all the 'sleazes' in the play. MRS THRATCHET had an affair with MR WOLF and SALLY THRATCHET is their 'love child'. I intend to make the comment that while SALLY THRATCHET may have suffered because her mother had an affair she does still idealise the romantic relationship her mother had. I do not wish to imply that there is any form of relationship between SALLY THRATCHET and MR WOLF, as it is revealed that he is her father and it would be far too incestuous. WINDOW WASHER is a male pig. He is that construction worker who always whistles at every girl who walks past, and that every other girl ignores or swears at.

MR WOLF

MR WOLF is very smooth, dressed in a blue suit. He can charm anything and anyone. He has a real Broadway – Frank Sinatra style that affects anyone who so much as looks at him. He is not a deep character, he has no motivation that has any meaning. Instead he just lives and breathes charm. At the end of the play, his charm subsides to a good-looking, slightly feminine normality.

NB: The other characters in *A Huff and a Puff* are two-dimensional and are only there to make MR WOLF look particularly smooth and charming. They are larger than life.

The Stage and Set

Two Lumps, No Sugar can be altered to fit any stage. However, I have written it with a certain stage and setting in mind. As a result many of the stage directions are best suited to this particular stage.

I envisaged a proscenium arch stage. The stage itself proceeds a little beyond the archway. It thrusts into the audience just enough to have a rostrum far stage left in front of the archway. It is so far left that it does not at all interfere with the main section of the stage. There are curtains that can be opened or closed, that block off the main area of the stage, leaving the small thrust area free. Centre stage there is a set of stairs that lead down into the audience. It is possible to walk from the rostrum to the stairs, still on the section of the stage that thrusts past the archway. There is a centre aisle that leads to a door at the very back of the room, and a door halfway through the audience on the right (audience's right, looking at the stage). The arch itself is very large. Halfway up on either side is a balcony, big enough for at least one person.

The setting can be as ornate or as plain as desired. The play requires minimal props and sets, but there is certainly opportunity for them. *One Perm or Two* could be performed using a very detailed hairdresser's set, *Domestic Life* is written to be performed using a realistic lounge room setting, but how detailed or realistic this is can be altered. *The 69th Floor*, which uses the balcony could have a backdrop of a cityscape, and *A Huff and a Puff* could incorporate a detailed set of a comic, Broadway-like street. Alternatively all scenes could be performed with simple black boxes and ordinary chairs. The only specific detail of the setting that is required is a bookshelf situated beside the rostrum. This can be as ornate or plain or unrealistic as desired, but some of the books must be real. There must also be a very large book on the rostrum. Once again, the exact appearance of the book is left to the director's discretion.

The Undefined Character

Somewhere out there, there must be more. More than there is here. Wherever here may be. Perhaps I am just too lonely for my own good. But one thing is for sure, out 'there' there must be more. More than you can ever dream of. Dream, dream ... now there is an elusive term. Did you as a kid ever think that maybe everything was a dream and that the only real thing was when you were dreaming? Or did you think that there was some giant somewhere that was just playing with all the people like over-sized Barbie dolls? Not God though, no, it was never God that I thought about. I remember when I was little, when I'd go to church, I used to think that Jesus lived behind the organ pipes. Must be cold and lonely back there I used to think. I comforted myself by being sure that he must go out sometime to get bread and milk and cheese. A stupid thought I guess but I am a fictitious character and can get away with anything. I wish I had a defined character. I mean what am I? Am I young, or old or somewhere in between? I bet you can't even tell whether I am male or female. I mean, is this a girl saying lines that belong to a boy or a boy saying lines that belong to a woman. Do you find me attractive? Is there any point, after all I could be gay ... but that could just make it even more appealing—especially if you stick me with this gorgeous specimen in the front row and throw in a pot of honey. But perhaps I am otherwise accounted for or really not your type anyway. One thing is for sure I am a fool and a lonely one at that. (*By now, MASTER OF CEREMONIES has reached the stage. In a pile to the left of the stairs are the clothes that he puts on.*)

But I do have a purpose here tonight, or this morning—perhaps just today is safer. (*Puts on top hat*) I am here to help you (*puts on tuxedo jacket*). How many times have you heard that one before. (*THE MASTER OF CEREMONIES is passed a cane from behind the curtains.*) Thank you. I am your Master of Ceremonies. I am here to take you through the wonders of a fictitious world. Never for a moment think it is real. It is not. It resembles reality, but that is only because you no doubt live in the midst of it. The person next to you is real. I am real. And let me assure you, on all accounts you are real. Unfortunately you, me and the person next to you are alone, so please do not take anything too seriously. I am your guide, your representative, your friend.

MASTER OF CEREMONIES walks to Stage Left. At the front is a rostrum with a very large book. Next to the rostrum is a large bookcase. Most of these books can be false, although at least two must be real. MASTER OF CEREMONIES opens the book on the rostrum at a place marked with a very large bookmark.

MASTER OF CEREMONIES: (*Curtains to main stage start to open*) Somewhere in the outskirts of Northern England, in a village that doesn't exist, at least not beyond the minds of the fictitious characters that inhabit it, there were a lot of lonely people. (*Behind the curtains, OLD WOMEN sit down in a straight line facing the front. They start to mime: instructing hairdressers, picking out magazines and generally settling in. This is done in freeze frames that fit in with the rest of THE MASTER OF CEREMONIES' dialogue.*) There were also a lot of foolish people. (*Freeze*) This is the tale of loneliness and the fools that it attracts. (*Freeze*) Or maybe it is the tale of fools and the loneliness they attract. (*Freeze*) Either way, it is a tale of some kind ... although, perhaps it is a lesson—one that can be forgotten.

* * *

One Perm or Two?

Beryl:	Have you seen Mrs Thratchet's new hair?
Mavis:	Oh, yes.
Maud:	I can't believe she did it.
Mrs Headlow:	I can. Always been a strange one she has.
Beryl:	Always up to no good as a girl.
Mavis:	Oh, yes.
Maud:	I can't believe she did it.
Mrs Headlow:	Always a friend of the boys, if you know what I mean. Still is by the looks of things.
Beryl:	So I've noticed!
Mavis:	Oh, yes.
Maud:	I can't believe she did it.
Mrs Headlow:	Boots up to her knees.
Beryl:	And skirts hardly covering her waist.
Mavis:	Oh, yes.
Maud:	I can't believe she did it.
Mrs Headlow:	She has only been married once though. No commitment, that's her problem.
Beryl:	I felt sorry for that Mr Thratchet. She has had so many children and not a single one looks like him—and he was her *only* husband you know! It seems she took his name and everything else he had, including his heart, never been the same after she left him, poor fellow.
Mavis:	Oh, yes.
Maud:	I can't believe she did it.

Mrs. Headlow: He was a nice fellow. Always smiling you know, but not in that suspicious way that so many young people smile nowadays.

Beryl: Although that Mr Wolf she gallivanted around with for a while seemed quite a gentleman. We need not ask what made him lower his otherwise high standards to the likes of Mrs Thratchet. He certainly was a gentleman —the type that does peculiar things to one's body temperature and breathing pace.

Mavis: Oh, yes.

Maud: I can't believe she did it.

Mrs Headlow: Oh, I know. Although, I have been told Mrs Thratchet has her ways.

Beryl: It is the children I really feel sorry for though.

Mavis: Oh, yes.

Maud: I can't believe she did it.

Mrs Headlow: Poor little things. Each looks so different and not one looks like poor Mrs Thratchet's abandoned husband.

Beryl: No. Not a single one. Although one does look like Mr Edwards the milkman.

Mavis: Oh, yes.

Maud: I can't believe she did it.

Mrs Headlow: I have a good mind to write a letter of complaint I have.

Beryl: Yes, but who would deliver it? Little Tommy Thratchet looks so much like Mr Wording, the mailman. And I saw her with him the other day ... talking ... in the front garden.

Mavis: Oh, yes.

Maud: I can't believe she did it.

Mrs Headlow: Well, I could get Mr Fromton, the baker, to deliver it.

Beryl: No, I wouldn't if I were you. Sally Thratchet has brown eyes very like his you know.

Mavis: Oh, yes.

Maud: I can't believe she did it.

Mrs Headlow: True. Maybe Mr Tooking, the butcher, could deliver it after work one day.

Beryl: Yes, he could, but Samuel Thratchet is a very tall boy ... and who else do we know who is very tall?

Mavis: Oh, yes.

Maud: I can't believe she did it.

Mrs Headlow: Perhaps Rev. Minding could hand it to her after church on Sunday?

Beryl: I don't know, the twins Cecelia and Amelia Thratchet both have a nose that is very much like that of Rev. Minding.

Mavis: Oh, yes.

Maud: I can't believe she did it.

Mrs Headlow: It seems that no man in the village has been safe from the wants of Mrs Thratchet.

Beryl: No. It is terrible what a woman can do to a village of otherwise self-respecting men.

Mavis: Oh, yes.

Maud: I can't believe she did it.

Mrs Headlow: Well that is what comes of being a single woman living a lonely life. She is not married any more you know.

Beryl: Oh yes, I know. I am very glad to say I am not a lonely woman, I don't know what I would do without my dear Albert, it is always a comfort to know he is always sitting there, in front of the wireless. I mean is it any wonder she does *That* to her hair!

Mavis:	Oh, yes.
Maud:	I can't believe she did it.
Mrs Headlow:	Well I suppose Mrs Thratchet's present situation is all the result of questionable parentage.
Beryl:	I remember her family, her mother was always wearing trousers ... not slacks, and her father was ... an accountant.
Mavis:	Oh, yes.
Maud:	I can't believe she did it.
Mrs Headlow:	Mrs Alsworth who lives in number 37 told me that her friend Mrs Epping was talking to her sister's nephew-in-law who told her that a friend of his once saw Mrs Thratchet's father at the track. Betting. On horses.
Beryl:	Doesn't surprise me. Not at all.
Mavis:	Oh, yes.
Maud:	I can't believe he did it.
Mrs Headlow:	It is disgusting what some people get up to in their spare time.
Beryl:	Yes, they have no thought for others and the impression they might be giving.
Mavis:	Oh yes.
Maud:	I can't believe you just said that.

(Curtains begin to close again)

* * *

Master of Ceremonies:	Mrs Thratchet was certainly a victim of this lonely world. Why? Well that is a common question. Despite the neighbours' opinions, she came from a good home and went to school and did all the things that one must do in order to fit a statistic.

As the sun hides its smile from the truth of the daylight, Mrs Thratchet, an actor of sorts and a mother of many, nurtures her developing lung cancer.

Her many children dance around her head. Many children who are, were, and most probably will be unwanted. This modern mother earth ponders her existence, the meaning of life and why anyone ever thought of creating a meal that is halfway between breakfast and lunch.

Time is of the Essence

Mrs Thratchet

Time is of the essence. Time is passing me by. I went to buy some milk the other day, but it had passed its use-by-date. I knew how it felt. It seems to me that we are squeezed into this world—dragged screaming and kicking and then thoughtlessly thrown into nappies. We are then forced to suck on some woman's breast—something men never seem to get over. Then as if that is not enough we are paraded around like giant dolls, wearing larger than life pink bows. Next we are abandoned into pre-school as some kind of warning of the inevitable torment of what is soon to come. School. The home of all childhood traumas. Your mother yanks and pulls your hair into pigtails in the vain pursuit of being 'cute'. You soon get to school where being cute only serves as amusement for the opposite sex who strut around in crew-cuts with obscure ears violently projecting in a style that has only ever been pulled off by Mickey Mouse. So you pull out your pigtails, only to get home and find your mother in tears at the disappointment that stands before her. Before you know it your hair has turned purple, your mother has given up and those goddamn 'members of the opposite sex' have let their hair grow long. To make matters worse, they now are particularly interested in what exactly lies behind that 'cute' front of yours. Before you know it you are sitting in the midst of a dark room regaining consciousness only to find your parents have a divorce, your friends have left you and there is some strange person lying next to you with their hand on your arse. And all this happened because your mother made you wear pigtails. *(She takes a long draw of her cigarette.)* In my opinion they should just leave us where we were all happy. In the womb. But I suppose then no one would ever be born and everyone would be all alone. Or would we? I mean if everyone was still inside someone else then the whole world would exist as one entity. All inside one giant woman. It would do an awful lot of good for feminism. *(Cigarette)* Stilettos. Who the hell ever thought them up? Men. Naturally. It takes a man to think of something truly ridiculous. If it weren't for men, I wouldn't have half a million midgets following me around. *(MRS THRATCHET sighs and resumes her cigarette and exits through the door at the very back of the audience. She moves slowly while the MASTER OF CEREMONIES speaks.)*

* * *

MC: A dream is no more than strange and confusing images designed by your mind to thoroughly confuse you. In this small village lonely dreams fill the night as admirable fools make no sense.

MASTER OF CEREMONIES turns to the bookcase and removes a small, dark blue book. He places it on top of the large book on the rostrum and opens it. Then, TOMMY THRATCHET enters stage left, in front of the closed curtains as MASTER OF CEREMONIES speaks. TOMMY THRATCHET is wearing blue and white checked pyjamas and carrying a Teddy Bear. He stares round the stage and at the audience, looking quite daunted. Then freezes, staring at the audience as he is described.

Young Tommy Thratchet tossed and turned as he dreamed a metaphorical dream. A lonely dream. Loneliness is contagious. Mrs Thratchet believed her children to be her curse, the truth is, she was theirs. But at nighttime this was no problem for Tommy Thratchet. He had all the entertainment he needed, locked away in his mind, just waiting to be released. (*The curtains open. TOMMY puts down the Teddy Bear, and sits him up so the Teddy is looking at him. TOMMY starts to put on a headdress, sitting centre stage. The headdress is made to look like the eyes and feelers of a fly.*)

* * *

Domestic Life

TOMMY THRATCHET as FLY moves to centre stage and sits on a 'wall'. ('Wall' may be interpreted in any way. My suggestion is that it is a rectangular platform that actually resembles a wall, as it is not a very important detail and may confuse the play.) The rest of the stage is set to look like an ordinary lounge room. There is an armchair stage left and a coffee table slightly off centre, toward stage right. On the table is a vase of flowers. There is a tall standing lamp far stage right and there is a rug on the floor. Any other details may be included. The aim is that the set looks homey, comfortable and ordinary. SALLY THRATCHET as CAT, wearing a full cat suit, is situated somewhere in the audience. She has her own seat in the audience. She sits preening herself until she enters. MASTER OF CEREMONIES remains behind the rostrum stage left.

Whilst speaking MASTER OF CEREMONIES takes the book and moves to the front row of the audience, sits down and 'reads'.

MC: In the great mansion of life, in a street of eternity, in the outer suburbs of probability, a Fly sat on a wall. It gazed at the world as it passed by, and pondered the meaning of life as various people made toast. Many people say that they would love to be a fly on the wall, but the truth is, it is not all that it is cracked up to be.

Fly: Ah me,

MC: Sighed the fly.

Fly: I see everything of everyone else's life—but nothing ever happens in mine. Nothing at all. This is my 21st birthday and my last day on earth. You see the average adult housefly only lives for 21 days, according to that fellow they were watching the other night on television. 21 days, that's all! And even that's only if there is adequate heat and light, and various other things that I never realised I needed. There is so little that I have done. There is even less that I still have to do. I haven't achieved anything. All I do is watch people eat. The people who live here always seem to be eating. I'll never understand it. The little ones are all sticky and covered in sugar and God knows what else. Every time I land on one of them, I can never be sure I'll be able to get off. As for the 'master of the house' well ... The thing that no one knows about him is that when no one's looking he reads Jane Austen novels. I suppose that's the advantage of being a fly on the wall, you see everything. Although if people realised everything included grown men crying over Mr Darcy, I really think they would change their minds. I quite like the mother of the family though, when she's not trying to swat me with anything that is. Oh, God I'm bored.

CAT sighs a very loud and dreamy sigh. She slowly gets up and makes her way toward the stage. FLY watches in a confused amazement. CAT continues to yawn as if she has just woken up from a very deep sleep. She slinks her way to the stage, stretching and sighing as she goes. She stretches out across the armchair, then turns to the fly who is looking at her with great curiosity.

Cat: What *are* you doing?

Fly: I don't know.

MC: Replied the Fly, and it was true, he had no idea what he was doing.

Cat: Why do you sit and stare?

MC: Inquired the Cat. She was always sticking her nose into other people's milk, and business, but mostly milk.

Fly: Because I have nothing else to do.

Cat: Nothing? Nothing at all? Why not? There is always *Something* to do. Something always has to be done.

Fly: Not for me.

MC: And the fly sighed and wiped a tear from his eye.

Cat: Well don't cry. It does not become you to feel sorry for yourself—only people who have no reason to feel sorry for themselves can truly get away with that. I am sure that if you thought very hard you could think of something to do.

Fly: I doubt it.

Cat: Come on. You must be good at something. Can you sing?

Fly: Oh yes. Very well. But every time I try to sing to someone, they shoo me away.

Cat: Well, can you dance?

Fly: No. I leave that to people who have reason to celebrate.

Cat: Are you good with people?

Fly: Not really. This morning I tried ever so hard to be friendly. I flew right down to the table and everything. But the people just yelled and tried to hit me with pieces of plastic. I tried to explain that I had no idea that what I landed on was edible, let alone 'little Freddy's birthday cake', but no one listens to me.

Cat: So you can't sing because no one will listen, you can't dance because you have nothing to celebrate and you have no people skills. You are right. You are pathetic.

Fly: Oh yes, I know. But I have never had any opportunities. I mean, what is on offer for your average housefly? To get anywhere in this world it seems you need to have at least four legs and an awful lot of fur. I guess I must be pathetic.

MC: Then the Fly suffered from a severe change of heart—which proved to be quite a painful experience.

Fly: Well ... what about you? What do you do that is so interesting? All I have ever seen you do is sleep and ... well... clean yourself.

Cat: Prrrecisely. (*CAT gets up and moves across to the table where she sits on the corner and reclines backward.*) What I do is self-prrreservation and prrreening. How else do you think I look so good?

Fly: I don't think you look very good at all.

Cat: No? (*CAT sits upright.*)

Fly: No.

Cat: Why not?

Fly: I don't know, I guess you're just not my species.

MC: One thing you must remember and never forget—not even late at night, is that you must never criticise a Cat's appearance. They are quite proud and distressingly sensitive. One comment slightly to the left of flattery and, if fashion requires it, they will escape to lead a life of anorexia.

Cat: Well, I don't think that you, with your spindly little legs and bulging eyes are anything to be prrroud of.

Fly: I will have you know that many a young Fly has fallen in love with this body of mine.

Cat: Rrreally?

Fly: No. But sometimes I think that if I pretend ... then maybe, just maybe it will be true.

Cat: No, I am afraid with a waistline like that, it will never be true.

Fly: You're probably right.

Cat: I am always right. That is the beauty of being a Cat, you are never wrong.

Fly: Or at least you never think you are wrong—that is the beauty of being egocentric.

Cat: What?

MC: Unfortunately, a Cat cannot deal with too many syllables in one sentence. That is their downfall.

Fly: You may be beautiful, but you don't understand a word I say.

Cat: I only don't understand it because I don't like it.

Fly: How do you know you don't like it if you don't understand it.

Cat: I understand that I am wasting my time talking to you (*CAT gets up and moves to stand centre stage, looking awkwardly out to the audience.*) ... I could be ...

Fly: Sleeping?

Cat: Yes. (*CAT moves back to the armchair.*)

Fly: I may be pathetic but so are you.

MC: The other thing you must always remember and never forget—even late at night—is never tell a Cat the truth. The pair stared at each other in silence.

Fly: In fact I bet you are even more pathetic than I am.

Cat: I am sure I am not.

Fly: So what can you do?

Cat: I can do many things. Ask me something. Ask me anything.

Fly: All right. What is the square root of 469?

Cat: Ah.

Fly: You can't do everything.

Cat: I certainly can. I just can't do maths. It is a prrroven scientific fact that the only reason you need maths is to build a satellite; and, as neither you nor I are building a satellite at prrresent or are showing any signs of building one in the near future the question is both null and void.

Fly: Are you all alone?

Cat: What?

Fly: Are you all alone?

Cat: I am not answering that. In fact I am not talking to you (*CAT turns away from FLY and sits in the armchair 'properly' with her arms folded*).

Fly: So who are you talking to then?

Cat: Myself—it is the only intelligent conversation anyone can get around here.

MC: The Cat was certainly defensive. She was not happy.

Fly: Be careful not to be too intelligent—you may not like what you hear.

Cat: I shall do and say whatever I want.

Fly: Fine, but I don't see what that will achieve. You are just as pathetic as I am. You will never change. I will never change. I am stuck to watch this world for my whole life.

Cat: I wouldn't upset yourself too much, being a fly that won't be too long.

Fly: True. But you. You have nine lives to live, or waste as it seems you are doing.

Cat: Waste? Waste! What are you talking about! I do not waste anything! (*CAT approaches FLY who is still sitting on the 'wall'. She moves very close to FLY and the two stare at each other from an uncomfortably close position.*)

Fly: You don't achieve anything either.

Cat: Isn't that just a little bit hypocritical? (*CAT starts to back away.*)

Fly: Perhaps. But I have an excuse. No one ever believes or respects a fly. I am far too small to be taken seriously, far too socially unacceptable to be listened to. You have no excuse. Hence you are more pathetic.

Cat: (*CAT curls and slinks around the lamp.*) You think anyone listens to me? I may be able to attract the attention of anybody I desire, but it doesn't get me anywhere. I am far too cute to be taken seriously, far too beautiful to be listened to.

Fly: I doubt you have ever tried.

Cat: (*CAT moves back 'too close' to* FLY.) I doubt you have either.

Fly: I doubt you have ever even cared.

Cat: (*CAT steps closer to FLY.*) I doubt you have ever left that wall.

Fly: True. I am a victim of domestication.

Cat: You are a victim? You can fly away whenever you like. My ancestors ruled the world. They were worshipped and praised just as all cats should be. Now, all we do is chase balls of string and wear diamanté collars—not even real diamonds! As for the media coverage, well, you would think all we did was chase mice all day.

Fly: Well there is only one thing we can do.

Cat: What?

Fly: Escape together. With your beauty and my brains we could rule the world! I mean, two heads are better than one. Even if they are both completely empty.

Cat: That is a charming idea and I would love to, but it is almost suppertime, and I hate to cause a fuss, especially when fish is on offer.

Fly: Ah, maybe some other day then.

Cat: Yes, another day. Tomorrow perrrhaps. Tomorrow we shall rebel and take on the world. It will be the beginning of a beautiful friendship, or something like that.

MC: Of course, if you have the life expectancy of a Fly, tomorrow never comes. And so the pair sat, in a cat-like readiness ... waiting for something to happen. Anything to happen. *Something* had to happen—something always did.

(*TOMMY and SALLY freeze and the curtains close.*)

MASTER OF CEREMONIES returns to the stage, replaces the book in the bookcase.

* * *

MC: The original Mr Thratchet loved his wife. (*MR THRATCHET enters through the curtains with a chair. He places the chair centre stage—still only on the thrust area as the curtains are closed. He sits on the chair the wrong way around, facing the audience.*) Not an original thought, but he did. He worshipped the very ground she walked on, along with most of the rest of male population. But days come and go and always end in nights—good for some, not good for those who are all alone. Candlelight may be romantic, but only if it has a pretty face to shine on.

As Time Goes By

Mr Thratchet

When I met her she was young. She was beautiful. She could talk, she could dance and she did frequently, with many people. Too many people. So I called and asked her why and what and how and she cried and she said she loved me. Then we got married. She was passionate and every night was like a honeymoon. Until one night: she slept, she slept all night. So I cornered her in the kitchen and asked her why and what and how and she cried and she said she loved me. Then she got a career. She wore stockings and suits and cute little twists in her hair. She sold 'cosmetics', sometimes far away, sometimes too far. So I left a message with her company and she called me back and I asked her why and what and how and she cried and she said she loved me. Then we had a child. She was kind and loving and cared so much. Then she started to complain and avoid me. So she paid for a babysitter, took me out and then I asked her why and what and how and she cried and she said she loved me. Then we started living each day and each week and each month until one day she wasn't there. So I called and called until I found her. I asked her why and what and how and she said I never told her I loved her and so I lost her to a Mr Wolf.

(*MR THRATCHET picks up his chair and exits the same way he came.*)

* * *

MC: Daughters are plentiful. Well, at least they seemed to be for Mrs Thratchet. Sally Thratchet was not particularly special. At least she didn't think she was. And she thought an awful lot. (*The curtains open to reveal SALLY THRATCHET.*) She had also read Rapunzel six and a half times. (*SALLY hugs a book close to her chest and spins around in a circle.*) She dreamed of long hair, the big city and a small boy by the name of Peter. (*She stops spinning suddenly and loosens her grip on the book disappointedly.*) Not that she had any chance of having long hair, ever going to the big city, and the small boy called Peter was infatuated with Amy Hartworth who lived in number 57. But she did know one thing, the big city must be awfully big. She fantasised herself a thousand miles away but still trapped all alone ... (*MASTER OF CEREMONIES walks onto the stage and takes the book violently from SALLY THRATCHET.*)

* * *

The 69th Floor

SALLY THRATCHET, as GIRL moves up to the balcony on stage left. (If a balcony is not possible, then podiums will do, preferably raised.) She rests her chin on her hand and stares off into space. This happens while MASTER OF CEREMONIES speaks.

MC: In a dark street, in a dog-eat-dog world where skyscrapers reach for the thick layer of pollution and the average family has 2.5 children and a divorce, on the 69th floor of the tallest building, a pretty young girl sat. She sat and stared out of the window and dreamed of a life of freedom, shopping and artificial laughter. She had been trapped and condemned to stare out of that solitary window for five years. Even the calls of Harrods, Chanel and an expanse of shoe shops were not powerful enough to save her. The lift had stuck on the 13th floor, leaving her to lead a life of loneliness. You see, in this cruel commercial 'don't call us we'll call you' world, no one would come to fix the lift.

One day, as she stared out of the window, the girl heard a strange whistling sound. (*WINDOW WASHER, played by MR WOLF enters stage right balcony—or podium, and begins to mime washing windows. He wears a pair of overalls and a lot of padding so that he looks very different when he enters again as MR WOLF.)* She stretched as far out of the window as possible to try and see where this strange sound was coming from. The girl could not believe her luck, there, hoisted alongside the skyscraper precariously placed too close to her own, was a window washer.

Girl:	Hi there!
MC:	The window washer lost complete control of his ... bucket as he peered across to see the most beautiful thing his blue collar life had ever encountered.
Window Washer:	How ya' doin'?
MC:	Called back the window washer as he tried to be cool, calm and collected. He failed as he sent his rag flying down to the cars and people down below. People who were all awfully late for a very important meeting.
Girl:	I'm fine, although I could be better.
Window Washer:	Really? Errr ... anything I could do?
Girl:	I am sure there is very much you could do, although I doubt a man like you would have time for a little thing like me.
Window Washer:	Hey, windows are my specialty ... hows-a-bout I find you a window in my schedule.
Girl:	Oh, you.
Window Washer:	By the way ... is your father a thief?
Girl:	Why?
Window Washer:	Because he stole the stars from the sky and put them in your eyes.
Girl:	You are so sweet!
Window Washer:	Compared to your beauty, I am a lemon.

MC: After that last comment both parties were thoroughly confused.

Window Washer: So ... errr ... you wanna go for some dinner some time?

Girl: I thought you would never ask!

Window Washer: I thought you would never say yes ... when are you free?

Girl: How about tonight?

Window Washer: Tonight is great.

Girl: There is just one problem.

Window Washer: What would that be?

Girl: Well, the lift to my apartment is stuck and I can't seem to get out.

Window Washer: Don't you worry your pretty little head. I'll get my good friend Charlie
                         ... he'll fix it in no time. *Pulls out a mobile phone.* Charlie, you doin'
                         anything? That don't count as anything ... look if you come and do your
                         magic on this lift then you would never believe the pretty thing that
                         I might just end up doin'. Ya' know what I'm sayin'? ... oh yeah, we are
                         talking breakfast, lunch and dinner! Thanks a lot. *Puts the phone away.*
                         He'll have that done by seven ... I'll pick you up then?

Girl: I can't wait. (*WINDOW WASHER exits.*)

MC: The truth is, she could wait. She could wait an eternity and never even
                         think of that window washer ever again.

                         In no time at all, although to the girl it felt like an age, quarter to seven
                         came, Charlie left and the lift was fixed. As the girl sailed to her freedom,
                         she thanked God for late-night shopping.

*SALLY THRATCHET exits. She then returns to the main stage and snatches the book from
MASTER OF CEREMONIES and walks off hugging it. Curtains stay open.*

* * *

MC: Sally Thratchet, the result of a very passionate, very brief and very illicit
        liaison. The very liaison that ended Mrs Thratchet's marriage.

        Music please. (*Some lounge chair jazz starts to play. It is soft whilst
        MASTER OF CEREMONIES speaks, but grows louder during the movement.
        The music must match the action on stage.*) Mrs Thratchet was a happily
        married woman, if such a thing is possible. She was loyal, caring, devoted
        and was always willing to scramble some eggs. Then one day, something
        caught her eye. A young 'gentleman' by the name of Mr Wolf. He was
        smooth, proud and always pursued his prey. In this case, the young,
        pure, innocent and above all married Mrs Thratchet was the object of his
        affection. The object of his lust. Or quite simply his object.

A Huff and a Puff

Mr Wolf

*MR WOLF is standing back centre stage. He is holding a cane and wears a hat—Broadway
style. The stage is black except for a spotlight on him. He is wearing a blue tuxedo. Although
under these lighting conditions he should appear like a silhouette. He looks up, clicks his
fingers and walks forward four steps. He stops, takes hold of his hat, tweaks the brim and
struts further toward the audience. At centre stage he turns side on, with his right side
facing the audience. He holds the peak of his hat again and slides his right foot in a circular
motion, and turns facing the audience again. He then rolls his hat down his arm and clicks
his tongue as if to say 'hey there' to the audience as he places the hat back on his head.
Three giggling girls dressed in 1950s, brightly coloured dresses enter stage right and freeze
about three steps away from him. He looks at them, smiles and nods his head. The girls let
out an enormous shriek/giggle and excitedly exit. MR THRATCHET enters stage left dressed in
a brown business suit. He shakes hands with MR WOLF, then they both slap each other on the
back and hug. MR WOLF clicks his fingers and points at MR THRATCHET with a small grin on*

his face. MR THRATCHET exits stage right with a look of 'what a guy' on his face. A young girl runs on stage from the audience and bumps straight into MR WOLF. She is dressed in a very stereotypical dress, with large bows in her hair. MR WOLF picks the girl up just as her mother runs on to scold her. She is dressed in a very plain dress. MR WOLF smiles at the mother who smiles back, he then hands the little girl a lollipop from his pocket. Both the mother and the little girl exit stage left. MRS THRATCHET enters stage right carrying shopping. She appears younger than before and is dressed in a white dress with a pink sash around her waist. He hair is carefully pulled back. She carefully walks past MR WOLF not paying any attention to him. She is walking out of time with the music. MR WOLF does a melodramatic double take with his whole body and follows after her. He just manages to leap in front of her before she exits stage left. He produces a bunch of flowers. She looks bashful and pushes them away. MR WOLF lifts MRS THRATCHET'S head with his finger under her chin. She stares into his eyes and drops her shopping. She takes a few steps back in time with the music. MR WOLF maintains his position and walks with her. He takes her hand and she spins her away from him, he then twirls her into his arms, both characters facing the audience. Together they walk forward. MRS THRATCHET looks back at MR WOLF and he dips her as low as possible. MRS THRATCHET is rigid at first, but then relaxes and lets her whole head drop back. She then shakes her head and her hair falls out of its neat arrangement. He pulls her back up, they stare at each other for a while and then kiss passionately. MRS THRATCHET then leads MR WOLF off stage right. They exit. MR WOLF reaches back on stage to retrieve MRS THRATCHET'S shopping, But MRS THRATCHET grabs him from off stage and he stumbles back off stage. The music ends.

MC: Thank you. That is quite enough. (*The music stops.*) A fling is a fine thing. Well, it rhymes so it must be true. The truth is, it is only true if both parties agree. Mr Wolf had a very well-rehearsed routine and Mrs Thratchet fell for it. She fell for it like a tonne of bricks, or perhaps a tonne of feathers, either way, she hit the ground, and left a pretty ugly mess.

Mrs Thratchet: (*Enters stage left*) Excuse me?

MC: Ah, yes?

Mrs Thratchet: Who the hell are you?

MC: I am your master of ceremonies, I am your guide, your representative, and
                       your friend.

Mrs Thratchet: Don't be ridiculous.

MC: *(Changing into a cockney accent)* Look, this is frightfully unprofessional.

Mrs Thratchet: I don't care.

MC: But ... ah, I'm here to tell your story.

Mrs Thratchet: My what?

MC: Your story.

Mrs Thratchet: What the hell are you talking about.

MC: Your story! How you came to be so unhappy, and lonely and disappointed
                       with your life. How you lost the one true love you ever had in this foolish
                       and lonely world. How your beauty faded and left you with nothing but a
                       lot of children you don't even want!

Mrs Thratchet: How dare you!

MC: *(Smugly)* But it's true isn't it.

Mrs Thratchet: No it's bloody well not.

MC: Oh, come on.

Mrs Thratchet: No I will not come on!

MC: Look, all I'm doing is telling the tale of loneliness and the fools it attracts
                       or fools and the loneliness they attract OK? To be perfectly honest I don't
                       care whether you screwed your life up or whether it was the result of this
                       cruel world ...

Mrs Thratchet: *(Punches MASTER OF CEREMONIES in the face knocking him over, he
                       swaggers, tries to steady himself on the bookshelf but knocks it down.*

He falls over with it—as close to the centre of the stage as possible. He remains on stage, unconscious.) Don't you dare tell me that my life is screwed up! I am a happy mother and I do what I can for my children. I have even had a career, a beauty consultant I was, in the big city—did you mention that? No! It took my ex-husband to mention that! As for implying that he is 'my one true love'! Well, don't even get me started! I mean, I may complain about my life, the state of the world and the general male population—but that just makes me a woman, which is coincidentally the complete opposite of both a failure and a man. This whole thing has been a complete defamation of character! I grant I may have made some mistakes in the past, but at least I don't feel I have to haunt the bloody world being poetical and giving running commentary on other people's lives.

Mr Thratchet:	*(Enters stage left)* What the hell is going on ... who on earth is that!
Mrs Thratchet:	Some 'Master of Ceremonies' or something.
Mr Thratchet:	What do you know.
Mrs Thratchet:	He thinks you're a right git. Pining over me and moping about the ways of love. All based on the way you tell the way our marriage ended.
Mr Thratchet:	Poor misguided fellow.
Mr Wolf:	*(Enters stage right)* There you are, I've been looking for you all over the place ... who the hell is that.
Mr Thratchet:	Some ceremonial creep.
Mr Wolf:	Ah, the artistic sort then.
Mr Thratchet:	Yeah.
Mrs Thratchet:	*(Looks at her wristwatch)* Oh, look at the time, I've got to pick the children up from school.
Mr Thratchet:	Oh, yes, we have to get home too.

Mr Wolf:	*(Putting his arm around MR THRATCHET and then sliding it down onto his bottom)* Yes, we have to look at those wallpaper samples ... are you still coming for dinner on Thursday night?
Mrs Thratchet:	Oh yeah! I may bring Tommy with me though, he has been having some strange dreams lately.
Mr Thratchet:	Oh really? Like what?

MRS THRATCHET, MR THRATCHET and MR WOLF exit stage left still talking. As they leave MAUD, MAVIS, BERYL and MRS HEADLOW enter and go back to their positions 'at the hairdresser's.' MASTER OF CEREMONIES remains unconscious.

Beryl:	Look at him just lying there.
Maud:	Oh, yes.
Mavis:	I can't believe she did it.
Mrs Headlow:	That is what you get for always commenting on other people's lives.
Beryl:	Yes it certainly is. He is quite nice looking though. I hope that Mrs Thratchet has not disturbed nature's picture.
Maud:	Oh, yes.
Mavis:	I can't believe she did it.
Mrs Headlow:	Do you think that there is anything that we can do?
Beryl:	Oh, I don't know ... he looks quite peaceful all unconscious like that.
Maud:	Oh, yes.
Mavis:	I can't believe she did it.
Mrs Headlow:	I guess he got what was coming to him. And who are we to get in the way of justice.

Beryl: That is a good point. One must never get in the way with things that
                    ought to be. Young Timothy Edwards found that out when he walked in
                    front of that bus that day. You must never get in the way of things that
                    have a set destination.

Maud: Oh, yes

Mavis: I can't believe he did it.

Mrs Headlow: No, it is best to let things end when they are designed to.

Beryl: Yes that is very true. It is a shame some people don't realise that.

Maud: Oh, yes

Mavis: I can't believe it.

Mrs Headlow: Well he was a very poetical sort of chap.

Beryl: Yes. It is no wonder that he ended up unconscious.

Maud: Oh, yes.

Mavis: I can't believe she did it.

Mrs Headlow: I wonder if now he has found what he was looking for.

Beryl: You mean whatever more it was that was out 'there' and not 'here'?
                    Maybe he has, still, I think Mrs Thratchet could have found a better way of
                    showing him.

Maud: Oh, yes.

Mavis: I can't believe she did it.

Mrs Headlow: Well, never mind. There is very little that we can do about it now.

Beryl: Hmm. We are ever so busy nowadays. They say that the twilight years are
                    the most peaceful, I don't agree. I'm run off my feet what with shopping
                    and getting my hair done and everything else we have to do. I mean, here
                    we are, people think we are just getting our hair done but truth be known
                    we are solving everyone's problems for them. If only they would listen

to us then the world would be a less lonely and foolish place. But does anyone listen to us? No. All our good day's planning will go unnoticed, completely behind other people's backs and over their heads. I mean, we have sorted out the problems and conspiracies of almost everyone in the village today, but do they realise the good we do?

Maud: Oh, no.

Mavis: I can't believe we did that.

The Food of Survival

There is nothing here. There is no point in going on. There is no reason for living. Vegetables are given no chance.

When was the last time you heard of a carrot getting a five-minute start? Vegetarians are the cruellest people ever to set foot on this Earth. Every harvest is a massacre and they think that they are being kind. Mass murder every Autumn. They are found innocent with no trial and our families fall at their mercy.

We have stayed quiet for long enough, fellow Vegies. We have been the victims of *Alternate Living* for long enough. It is time to fight. To pick up our roots and go into battle.

Who is with me? Oh, my irrigated soil for a van. My Fertiliser for an army and my Scarecrow for ammunition. We must fight.

> This day is called the feast of Crispy-Lettuce
> The vegetable that returns to the field safe,
> Will grow tall when this day is named,
> And flourish at the name of Crispy-Lettuce.

Kat and Jenna performed many Shakespearean pieces together.

He that shall live this plough,

And see Wilting age,

Will scorn his neighbours who return to feast on Vegetables,

And say 'Tomorrow—is Saint Crispy Lettuce',

He shall tell the tale of our battle and our names

Familiar in his mouth as farmyard words—

Harry the Carrot, Bedford the Bean,

Exeter the Brussels sprout and Warrick the Broccoli.

From this day to the ending of the Farm,

We shall be remembered!

And the men in England who are now in bed,

Shall shiver at the thought of those vegetables who

fought at the battle of Crispy-Lettuce!

We cannot live as an Entree forever! We must Fight! Fight for the right to live. Fight for the right to grow. Fight for the right to be the Vegetables we are because they may eat our flourish but they'll never eat our freedom!

Only Blondes Prefer Gentlemen

A wise woman once said 'Diamonds are a girl's best friend' and boy was she right. After much consideration I have decided there is no point getting all holier than thou about it … Darling, if you want to talk bollocks and discover the meaning of life, you're better off downing a bottle of whiskey. At least that way, you're unconscious by the time you start to take yourself seriously.

I remember how I met Him. It was at some ghastly dinner and I had sat myself down beside Him—for obvious reasons, oh didn't I tell you? He owns or rather owned … a diamond mine... Things were not quite going as planned. We were halfway though the soup and … well … I had said precisely four words to the very rich gentleman on my left. I said, 'Isn't this soup delicious?'; that's four words.

And he said, 'Yes, isn't it?'; that's three. Quite disappointing … Even then though, there was something about him, other than his diamond mine, something that bothered me … I think it was his eye! Yes, it was this! He had the eye of a vulture—a pale blue eye, with a hideous veil over it. Whenever it fell upon me, my blood ran cold; and so by degrees—very gradually—Anyway … We were at dinner. Now darling, I *like* exotic food. But this particular dinner was ridiculous. You have to remember what they say, you are what you eat. Which made whoever hosted it a very large, vegetarian tart.

Now where was I? Oh yes, how we met. Well, when the fish came it all heated up a little. I thought I wonder if he likes fish? … Yes, he does; he says he likes fish. Ah, that's nice. I love that in a man. Now he's asking me if I like fish. Now does he really want to know, or is it just a line? I'd better play it casual. I'll tell him, 'Oh, pretty well'.

I like fish pretty well; there's a fascinating bit of autobiography for him to study over.

I wonder what else he likes. Does he like cucumbers? Yes, he does; he likes cucumbers. And potatoes? Yes, he likes potatoes, too. Why, he's a regular old Nature-lover, that's what he is. I would have to come to dinner, and find that the richest man in the room is nothing but a 'wanna-be' David Attenborough ...

From then on it was a diamond-studded dream. I had the best of everything! However ...

It is impossible to say how the idea first entered my brain; but, once conceived, it haunted me day and night. I loved the old man or at least I loved his fortune.

So it's not that it was a bad life. Not a bad life, darling. No, not such a bad life. Just a boring life. I thought to myself 'I can't sit here flicking through magazines all day. I can't live my life as if I'm at the bloody hairdresser, for heaven's sake!' I mean, I just felt like shouting out 'excuse me if I sue when I die prematurely of passive *boredom*!' I was living my life at a level of boredom that would make a battery *chicken* take up an evening class. I mean it's no wonder I started to think of such morbid ideas, I mean I knew it wasn't right ... So I tried to improve myself as a person—or something like that. ... I called my beauty and health salon and said: 'Cancel my aromatherapy, my psychotherapy, my reflexology, my osteopath, my homeopath, my naturopath, my crystal reading, my shiatsu, my organic hairdresser, and see if I can be rebirthed next Thursday afternoon.' And they said 'Consider it done.'

I even tried giving up drinking. Worst eight hours of my life.

It was no good. I had to do it. I had to kill him. Now this is the point. You fancy me mad. Madmen know nothing. But you should have seen *me*. ... I was never kinder to the old man than during the whole week before I killed him. Upon the eighth night I *felt* the extent of my own powers I fairly chuckled at the idea; and perhaps the old man heard me; for he moved in bed suddenly, as if startled and then he sprang up crying out—'Who's there?'

I kept quite still and said nothing. His eye was open—wide, wide open—and I grew furious as I gazed upon it. I saw it with perfect distinctness—all a dull blue, with a hideous veil over it that chilled the very marrow in my bones; but I could see nothing else of the old man's face or person. Then I heard this very irritating sound. *A low, dull, quick sound— much such a sound as a watch makes when enveloped in cotton.* It was the beating of the old man's heart. I increased my fury. The old man's hour had come! I threw my hands around his throat. But it wasn't good enough... 'Oh, for God's sake, *just die*!' and then he did.

Do you hear that? No? ... nothing? ... are you sure you don't hear that? No? It's *a low, dull, quick sound*—It's the beating of his hideous heart!

This is why diamonds are a girl's best friend you know ... *square cut or pear shape these rocks don't lose their shape* ... So, not a bad life. Not a bad life, darling. No, not such a bad life.

The Fool

He that has and a little tiny wit,
With a heigh-ho, the wind and the rain.
Must make content with his fortunes fit,
Though the rain it raineth every day.

Taking one's part that's out of favour. Nay, and thou canst not smile as the wind sits, thou'lt catch cold shortly. There, take my coxcomb. Why, this fellow has banished two on's daughters and did the third a blessing against his will. If thou follow him. Thou must needs wear my coxcomb. How now, My nuncle? ...

Mark it, nuncle:
Have more than thou showest,
Speak less than thou knowest,
Lend less than thou owest,
Ride more than thou goest,
Leave thy drink and thy whore, And keep in-a-door,
And thou shalt have more
Than two tens to a score. ...

'Tis like the breath of an unfee'd lawyer: you gave me nothing for't. Can you make use of nothing, nuncle? ...

Fools had ne're less grace in a year
For wise men are grown foppish,
And know not how their wits to wear,
Their manners are so apish.

I have used that nuncle, e'er since thou madest thy daughters thy mothers; for when thou gavest them the rod and puttest down thine own breeches,

> Then they for sudden joy did weep
> And I for sorrow sing,
> That such a king should play bo-peep
> And go the fools among

Prithee, nuncle, keep a schoolmaster that can teach thy fool to lie. I would fain learn to lie. ...

I marvel what kin thou and thy daughters are. They'll have me whipped for speaking true, thou'lt have me whipped for lying, and sometimes I am whipped for holding my peace. I had rather be any kind o' thing than a fool; and yet I would not be thee, nuncle. Thou hast pared thy wit o' both sides and left nothing I' th' middle. ...

Thou wast a pretty fellow when thou hadst no need to care for frowning. Now thou art an O without a figure. I am better than thou art, now. I am a fool; thou art nothing. Yes forsooth, I will hold my tongue; so your face bids me to do so, though you say nothing.

> Mum, mum
> He that keeps nor crust nor crumb,
> Weary of all, shall want some.
> That's a shelled peascod.

For, you know, nuncle,

> The hedge-sparrow fed the cuckoo so long
> That it's had its head bit off by its young;

May not an ass know when the cart draws the horse?

Whoop, Jug, How I love thee! ...

Tarry, take a fool with thee.
For a fox when one has caught her,
And such a lovely daughter,
Should sure to the slaughter,
If my cap would buy a halter.
So the fool follows after.

The Fool

*The Fool is a complex character in Shakespeare,
full of wit, insight and pathos.
And Kathryn captured all these qualities in her
dramatic portrayal of King Lear's fool.
She breathed life, and energy into a character who
was, at that time, mostly played by men and she
was captivating.
And so, it was with this monologue that her
fascination, exploration and relationship with Fool
commenced.*

Ms Thérèse Bennetts
Coordinator of Public Speaking (Internal)
Speech & Communication Teacher
Presbyterian Ladies' College, Sydney

*The Fool: Movement and words blended to build an
outstanding character. Exemplary use of props and
space—Full marks*

The Fool from ASCA Examiner's report Grade 8
25/11/1997 by Gillian Burgess

Fool's Costume made
as 'a body of work' for
Level 1 Art HSC

A note from Dangerous Liaisons producer

A Note from the Producer & Director

Kathryn Carter was incredibly excited about co-directing Dangerous Liaisons. She seemed happiest when she was slowly putting a play together, piece by piece. She loved the messy details of human feeling splashed all over the stage. She loved the raw exhibitionism of the theatre. It was all, like her, somehow larger than life.

Tragically, Kat fell ill and passed away before we could all enjoy a glass of champagne with strawberries on opening night. She never saw the finished play. We will always remember her as a young woman who loved and was loved.

She lit up the room when she entered it. She was the antidote to all that is bland, mean-spirited and loveless in the world. She was a poet, an actor and a thinker who loved her Dead White Male writers unashamedly. She had an infinite capacity for forgiveness and generosity. Life just could not be mundane when she was around. Instead, it had a flavour that was rich, strange and full of sparkly diamontes.

It is fitting that Dangerous Liaisons be Kat's final work. A work that truly reflected her being – complex but beautiful all at the same time.

Steve Dziedic (co-director)
Cat Prestipino (producer)

STORIES

The Phone

Everybody was playing in Cristerfer John's room when a terribble 'Ring Ring' Everybody ran and hid, Poo in the toy box, Tigger under a lamp shade, Rabbit in a shoe box, and Piglet behind a strange thing with a hat and a cord! 'Oh DDDDear' said Piglet 'iiits Illouder now!' Then Cristerfer John came running in and took of the 'Things hat' and talked to it but it only wisperd to Cristerfer John!

'What was that?' Poo asked Cristerfer John 'Silly old Bear it's a telephone!'

'OH' said everyone.

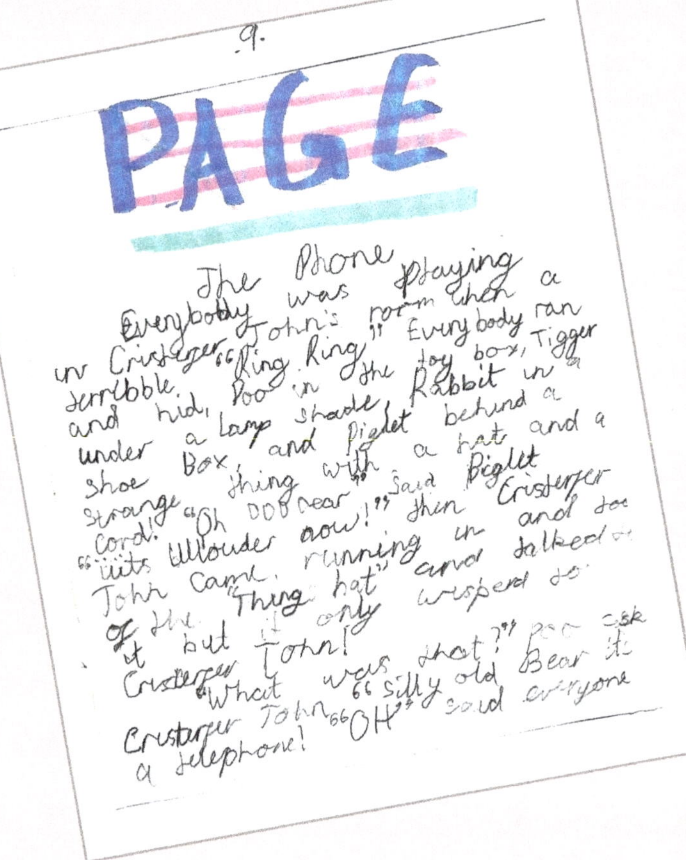

In the Beginning

I sat still and patient. There was nothing, no lights, no darkness, nothing outside the walls of my time machine. Suddenly there was a massive explosion and light was brought into exeistance. When my eyes ejusted to the new bright light I could see a small blue-green ball. Slowly as I ejusted more to the surroundings I could see that the green was land, one big mass Could this be the earth that I would soon live on?

I came down to land and looked from the window of my time machine. Reptiles, large thundering giants, obviously DINOSORS!! I was safe in the time machine and I watched intensavly. I knew that the dinosors were one of the later stages after algie and things. How could that be? Only 5 minutes ago I was watching the world being created.

A Dinasore fell and was followed by others. They were dieing! Their bodies lay there still and silent. Then came the rats! It was too much! I set the co-ordinents and left. I materilised not in my own Time but still there were humans. I re-set the machine and found myself back where I started looking down at the world. All of a sudden the big land mass split! It split and there was a noise like the bite of an apple!

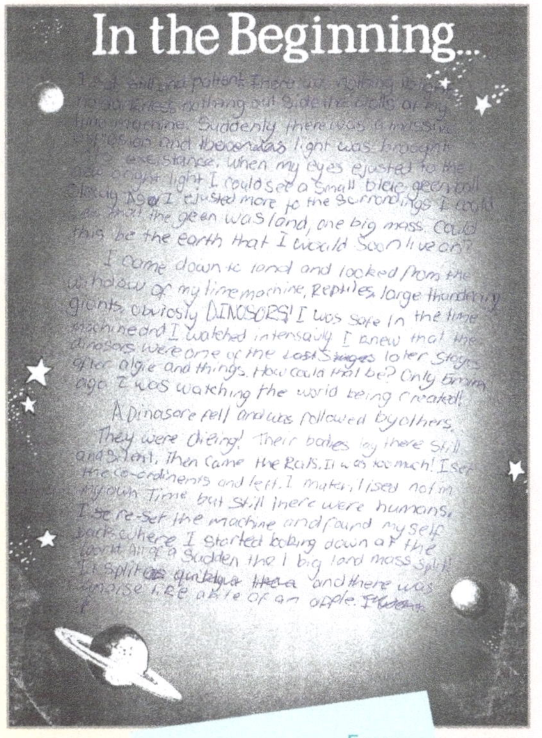

From
a primary school
scripture book

A Not Surprising Murder

CONTENTS

Chapter One

One night Helen and John Cart went to visit Jenny and Steven Que. Helen was tall and beautiful but selfish. John was obsessed with his work. John was bored with Helen. Jenny was tall, pretty but not at all selfish!

Steven was short, bald with a moustache. And I have [no idea] what Jenny saw in him.

The whole house was in a bad mood after Helen had been screaming about her broken nail!

John missed dinner saying 'My computer's frozen up!'

At dinner Helen sipped her wine then knocked over the rest so no one else could enjoy any! This made Jenny and Steven angry! And dinner was finished in stoney silence when they all went to bed!

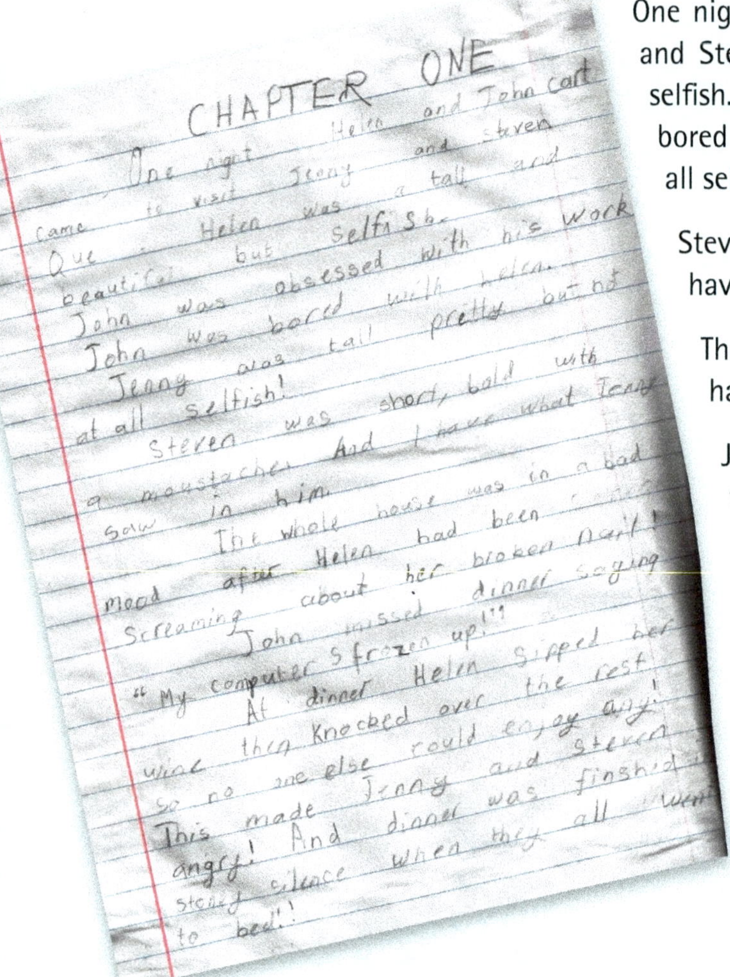

Chapter Two

Next morning Jenny came up to call Helen down for breakfast.

When she got up there and tried to wake up Helen she would not or could not move!

Jenny had studied nursing and checked her pulse, but there was no pulse!

So she ran downstairs and shouted 'HELEN IS DEAD!'

Chapter Three

Sergeant Harvey was called for!

Helen had been POISONED. Sergeant Harvey questioned John, Jenny and Steven.

He decided they all had a reason to kill Helen.

John was bored, Jenny was jealous and Steven was angry at how Helen treated Jenny!

He sat on an old red armchair to think.

He played with a loose button on the arm.

Suddenly the chair swung round and he was faced with a dark passage.

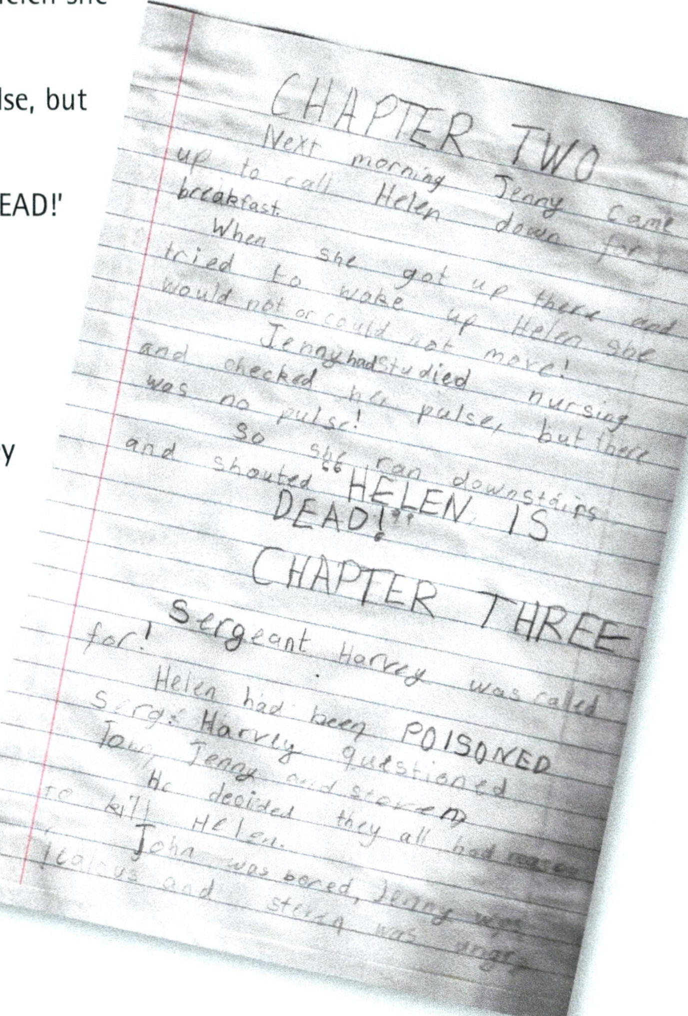

In a dark corner hidden was a small bottle of poison.

Carelessly dropped beside it was a gold lighter!

Serg. Harvey brought the lighter out into the light and [was] looking at it when Steven walked in.

'Oh you have found Jenny's lighter good show old chap!!!!'

WHO DID IT?

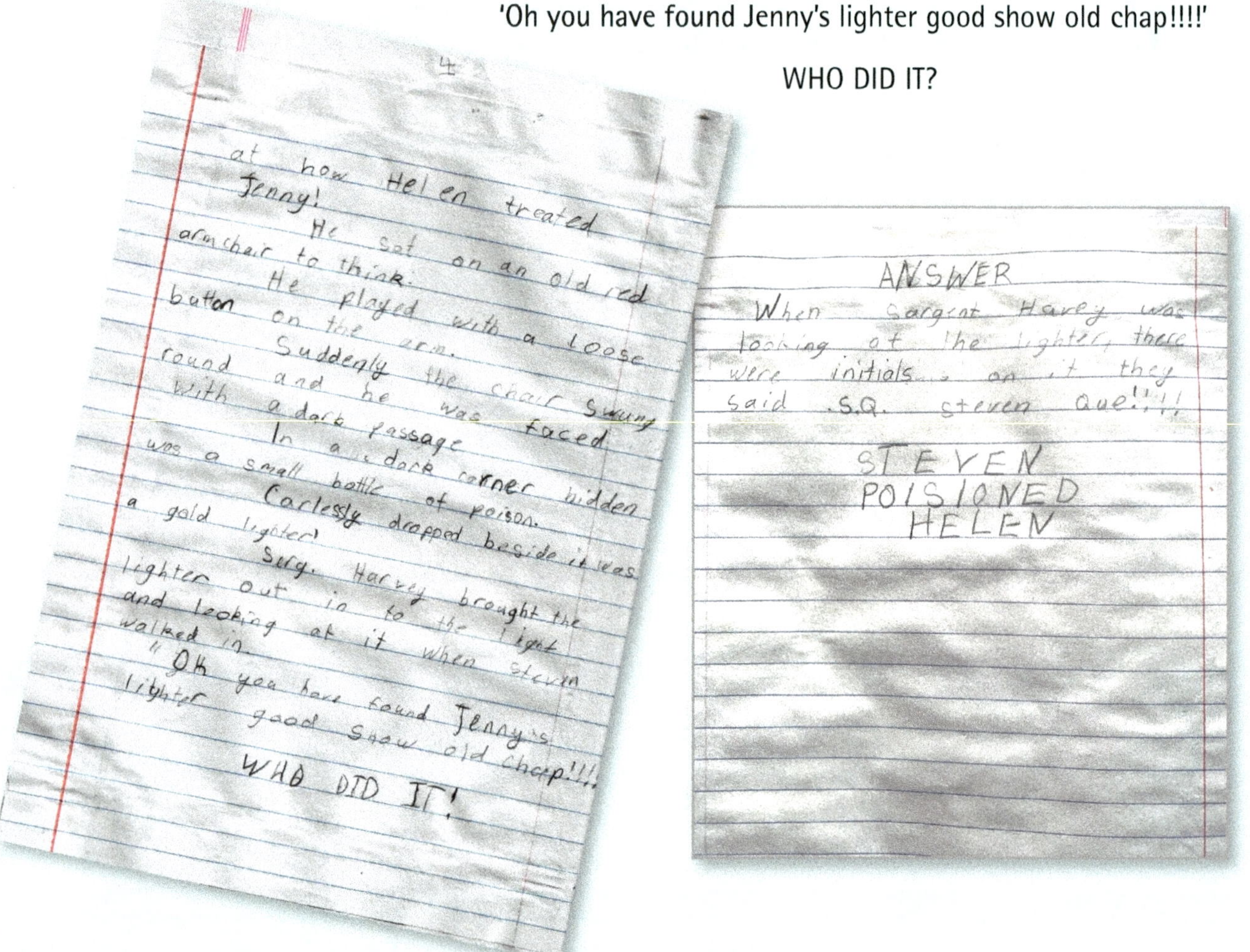

Christmas Puddings

In the North Pole in a secret place that only Father Christmas, Mother Christmas and the Elves know is a land called Puddington, where all the Pudding people live!

Pudding people, are, well, Puddings! They look just like Puddings rapped in cloth, and like the Puddings we eat they get better as they get older, wiser and they teach Pudlets how to read and write they also tell them about the legends of Christmas!

Some of the popular ones are; How Christmas Puddings were invented, What happend when Santa got sun stroke in Australia, The Time Jack frost stole santas slay and the doll that came to life and escaped from santas slay!

But the favourite of all the Pudlets is the one about the time when the good spirit of Christmas defited the bad Spirit of Christmas and locked him in a cage of ice that not be broken unless a full sugar Pudlet found the key and opend the cage on Christmas eve!

In Puddington there lived a girl Pudle named Pippi! Pippi was the most beautifut Pudding in whole of Puddington!

Everyone was jelse of her, but [one] Pudlet was perticuly jelouse! Her name was Penny, she was Pippi's sister! Pippi had beautiful long hair, dazziling looks and as

Picture given as Christmas present to her father and now used as the logo of J W Carter Publishing

if this was'nt enough she was made with no added sugar! And Penny could'nt stand her!

Pippi and Penny wernt the only Pudlets in their family, they had a brother called Peter. He was always up to no good!

On Christmas eve the Pudlets where boared, They had finished their pre-Christmas Dinner (Pudding People love their Christmas Lunch and have it several times befor Christmas!) and wrapping their Christmas prescents! (It's a Pudding Tradition to wreapp Presents on Christmas eve!) The Pudlets had been sent to bed.

They where so excited about Christmas they could'nt sleep and had nothing to do! Suddenly Peter had a fantastic idia to go out for a walk to see all the Christmas decorations! (Every Pudding person must put up Christmas decorations out the front of the house, if they don't the[y] can be chaged six sulanas for neglegence!)

Every Christmas eve they have a compitetion for the best decoratins! (Mr Plum, Peter, Pipi and Penny's Father had won it three years running!)

They started to walk, the Christmas cave where the ice cage was said to be held was'nt far from the village, about five minutes in a Raison-beel, but on Pudding it was about ten minutes! The Pudlets wobled and wobled untill finally the[y] came to the Christmas Cave.

Hidden among the Sunflowers

The teacher with her gold bracelets swaying gracefully rubbed the red chalk off the board unsuccessfully as the chalk just smudged. She then wrote up some maths questions, extremely boring! If there was one thing about the beautiful, elegant Miss Scarlet, who

had all the boys in stitches, it was that she was incredibly boring! Once she had finished writing the sums on the board, she sat on her chair without creasing her pleated skirt or her expensive silk shirt. She then started fiddling with her necklace and started flipping her brown leather sandals! She then (with her extremely blue eyes) glared at the class, her face sweet and expressionless. I was bored. I sat in the back row of the class (because Miss Scarlet had all her admirers in the front!) I had finished the sums and was watching a note being passed. Although Miss Scarlet was glaring at us, she was totally oblivious to what was going on!

The note finally reached me. No one ever read notes if not addressed to them because everyone was sending a note some time in their life and didn't like other people reading them (besides the person it was being sent to!) But everyone read the front of the folded note paper. I read it. 'Alex Pepergin' that was me! It went on to say on the front 'If you read this you will be cursed for life!!'

I opened out the folds, carefully flattening the recycled speckled notebook page as I went. When it was flat on my lap I read 'meet me at the sunflower bed after school'. I stared at the blonde ponytail belonging to Amy Peep in the front of me. Who sent me the note? There was no name at the bottom!

Finally, school was over so I walked with a few running spurts until I reached the sunflower bed. Among the golden heads on the great tall green stalks, I could just make out a pale figure facing in the other direction. So, I ran up and tapped the pale figure with long blonde hair like myself. She was dressed in unusual old-fashioned clothes. A pink frilly dress with a white lace pinafore. The girl turned. She had a sweet face, but she looked worried. Her eyes, green as the sea, and bright red lips! She smiled to show some yellow teeth with two gaps where her two front teeth should be. Then she vanished. I screamed. No one heard me. All the boarders were swimming, and I was a long way away from the classrooms.

I ran slipping on the grass. Then thumping on the cement. I grabbed my school bag, slung it on my back and ran home. Had I imagined that girl???

Testudo Elephantopus

He slowly pursues his journey. The short distance he must travel to get his food would be a mere step, hop and jump for anyone else but not for Thomas.

His wife has died, his friends have met their death, his children long gone without sparing a thought for their father. He is alone. His few possessions travel with him everywhere—a heavy load of memories.

People stare, look and wonder. Every one of his wrinkles has its own legend. But there is no one who can hear them or wants to hear them. He lifts up his head, an effort and not exactly worth it. Why must this heavy burden of life last so long?

There was a time when life was a new experience, when he had wanted to see everything, feel everything, touch everything, go everywhere and meet everyone. Now he had seen everything he wanted to see and a few other things! He had felt all he wished to feel. He had been everywhere he wanted to go and now he knew from experience he did not want to meet everyone.

Thomas's head is a gold mine of memories. Thoughts of standing on the edge of the beach, the sun slowly setting behind him mix with thoughts of swimming and long walks along the beach. Now these friends are gone, slowly passed him by—left him behind—he wants to follow them away from mortal life. Thomas desperately longs to join his wife and many of his children in whatever comes after the life he knew.

A wave of fatigue passes up Thomas's body to his head—he is tired, he has had enough and decides to retire to his shell for the night.

Letter

Simone McLennon

13 Penny Lane Strawberry Fields 9999

NSW Australia

Dear Simone

It is horrible, what I would give for a bath! All those years I took a good shave and a bath in the morning for granted. All those times I complained that the water was too cold—the way I am feeling I would have a bath in ice! Although I dare say that if I had any ice here the rats would be in it too! The thought that I may never see you again lingers in my mind—I miss you. In the cold dark nights when boredom sweeps across the trenches I think of home—how I long to be there, walk through the park as the autumn leaves fall, but no. I am here, sharing my so-called bed with the entire insect population. Although I fear you would run a mile should you see me. It has been at least 3 weeks since I had a good shave. Still, the candle has burned low and we need to conserve the small amount of light we have.

Yours forever
Robin Goodfellow xxooo

A Touch of Darkness

The sea was cool and gentle waves slowly rocked the boat, the smell of salt was in the air. Charlotte stood with her Mother with her long golden hair blowing in the wind and her blue dress blown against her legs while her Father, the Captain of the *Mary Celeste* walked ahead. His crew stood in a long line while he inspected them. Charlotte watched her Father as he walked with his head high in his regal uniform. They were going to Genoa, Italy. It was calm and they were all set to go. 'All aboard that's coming aboard from New York in the United States of America' called Simon the first mate and they set sail.

A Touch Of Darkness

The Mary Celeste was found by the crew of the Dei Gratia about half way between the Amazon and the Portuguese coast, they found the ship deserted although most of the provisions and equipment where still there. The only things missing were the Crew, the Captain and his wife and child, lifeboat and the navigation equipment.

All characters portrayed in this story are based on what the sailors back then may have been like .The sex of the Captain's child is not known to me and so Charlotte is a figment of my imagination.

Kathryn Carter

BIBLIOGRAPHY

The World Book Encyclopedia Volume M p. 240

That night there was a terrible storm and the boat was thrown about very severely. Everyone was sick, the men worked all night in the rain. Charlotte's mother Mary Celeste Tullach (the ship was named after her) said that it was the worst storm there had ever been. Mary tried to comfort her daughter Lotty (that was Charlotte's nickname). But Charlotte was sick and frightened, she shivered and perspired and she turned quite pale. It seemed that morning would never come!

Finally morning did come and the ship was a mess so Mary was expected to help clean up (being a woman!). They were all fixing up the mess that the storm had left when a lifeboat came drifting by. In it was a woman, she was very pale and sick. The crew assumed that she had been evacuated from a boat in the storm. The captain decided the natural decision, to bring her onboard and to take her to the Bones, the ship's doctor, which they did. Bones said that the woman was doing well and that she needed lots of rest, so they decided to keep her onboard, there wasn't anything they could do. It was funny, the lady had arrived on a lifeboat with the navigation equipment but the equipment was nowhere to be seen.

The boat and navigation equipment had just disappeared without a trace. No one made much fuss of it but everyone noticed that it had gone! Charlotte was suspicious of the woman but she didn't know why, it was just a funny feeling inside her.

The next day was perfectly normal except for the woman's extremely fast recovery. It turned out that her name was Miss Jasmine. Lotty still had a bad feeling about her. That night Lotty crept out of the cabin where they were living, she crept past her mother sewing in front of the fire and her father doing some paperwork at his desk. Soon she had passed the only threats to her escape and had left the cabin. Lotty crept down the corridor with her dressing gown wrapped tightly around her because it was so cold. Soon she came to the crew's mess. As she passed she heard laughing and singing. Lotty peeped in only to see the strange lady, *Miss Jasmine,* flirting with the crew! After all that fuss making *me* move out of my room she was going to spend all night with the crew! thought Lotty.

The next morning Lotty was woken up by people calling Sam, Sam, she got up and dressed quickly. Sam was one of the men that had been flirting with *Miss Jasmine*! He had just disappeared. All morning people searched but he was nowhere to be seen.

The next day three more of the crew disappeared, just no sign of them. More and more crew disappeared, some highly ranking mates had just disappeared. Then came the worst day, Lotty was just looking at the newspaper that her father had when she heard shouting. Lotty immediately ran out to see what was happening only to see Simon the first mate on the edge of the boat about to jump! Everyone was trying to coax him down, but no one could succeed. Lotty looked across at where Miss Jasmine was standing, she was smiling! David the second mate went up and stood next to Simon then Simon screamed and screamed and plunged into the water taking David with him! Lotty thought back to this morning, the strange lady Miss Jasmine whispering to him, then Lotty had an awful thought, she remembered Miss Jasmine talking to Father, then she said to herself 'No, no one can be killed from talking to someone? Can they?'

Peter was the next victim. The entire ship was slowly being eaten away by some evil power that was indescribable. The worst was yet to come. Paul caught from nowhere a deadly disease, his skin peeled, his hair fell out, he coughed and spluttered, his hands shrivelled up until all there was on them was skin with a green pigmentation. Bones spent all his time studying him working out a cure, but it was no good. Lotty watched through the keyhole, Paul slid one peeling hand down the doctor's face and then died. Lotty stepped back from the door anxiously with a sour expression when she was quite startled to receive a tap on the shoulder. Lotty turned and saw Miss Jasmine behind her. Lotty frowned at her. The strange lady replied 'Help me, it's my fault but it's not!' Lotty was worried and confused. The woman stuttered 'I—I—I can't help it, forgive me'. She wept 'You'll be next' then she reached out and touched Lotty on the shoulder then threw her arms around her. All of a sudden she stepped back and put her hands on her cheeks then Lotty noticed her eyes turn a shade of purple. The lady raised her eyebrows, lifted her head and walked off. Lotty ran back to her room. She was so confused and frightened that she started to cry. She slammed the door and ran to her room and threw herself on the bed, grabbed her doll and huddled up in a small ball with her head tucked down.

Soon Lotty had pulled herself together and proceeded towards the deck. On the deck the sails were being raised, the big sheets of canvas soon caught the wind, and they were sailing once again. Lotty headed towards the store room where the cargo of industrial alcohol was kept. There was a strong smell of alcohol around the area, Lotty peeped in the keyhole and saw Timothy *DEAD*. Lotty screamed. The encounter with Miss Jasmine flashed through her head. *You'll be next you'll be next* was going through her head over and over again. People rushed over to see what was the matter, they were all mortified they threw his corpse into the ocean. Bones contracted the disease that Paul had, and he died. Then the strange Miss Jasmine disappeared, Lotty saw her. She said 'My mission is over, my task is completed' and with that she disappeared. Father committed suicide. Mother disappeared. Soon it was only Lotty, no one else. The only thing she could think to do was to leave the ship that had caused all her sorrow so she let down the lifeboat, and something made her take the navigation equipment with her. Lotty sailed for days in the little lifeboat then she finally was about 10 metres away from the shore of an island when she turned the boat around and said, 'My mission has just begun!'

An Objective Opinion

She peered at the far horizon. The world really was a pretty place. She was really quite proud of herself. It is not easy to be in a situation like the one she was in and still be level headed enough to stop and objectively look at the world spin round. She was at a crossroad: two winding paths stretching ahead of her both promising different yet equally tempting things. The wind again hit her bare arms and a shiver ran up her spine. She closed her eyes and remembered how it was before. She could go back. Ignore all of this—pretend it never happened. Then she thought about it and realized that it had been a hard climb to get where she was and she was not keen to venture back down those rickety steps—back where it had started. At her command the whole situation could move on. At one command she could take the plunge into the unknown. She had come this far, it seemed stupid to turn back now. But was what she was doing simply stupid anyway? The whole philosophy of stupidity swamped her head. If she turned back now—how could she ever face *them* again. How could she lift up her head in public with the knowledge that her future was so close and yet she turned it down? How could she live with herself? It is one thing to be disappointed in another and to lose your respect and trust in them, it is another not to trust or respect yourself. She thought of all the thoughts she could never tell herself ever again and then realized how stupid she was being and then the irony of being stupid by thinking about stupidity hit her across the face. She took a deep breath. Decided it was now or never, let go, and slid down the slippery dip.

Two Green Lights

There's a Temple up the road from us, I wish there wasn't.

I walk to school every morning at eight o'clock. I can hear chants coming from the Temple up the road. Mum says that they are just welcoming the new day and that they're harmless. I'm not so sure.

One day I was walking past the Temple when curiosity got the better of me and I stood on my toes and peeked into the Temple. It was filled with oriental treasures—all on the theme of snakes! They were gold and encrusted with jewels. They were perfect and beautiful, every one of them. Suddenly a man entered the room, he didn't look at me at first, instead he turned to one of the snakes, the biggest, most beautiful one (with the most gold and jewels!). And he said a chant of some kind then he turned to me, his eyes were closed, I felt a choking sensation around my neck. He opened his eyes, two green lights glaring at me. I screamed and started to run, I ran and ran as hard as I could all the way home. As I ran in the door my mother greeted me with 'Hello Katy, what's that around your neck? Are you alright?' I wasn't really listening and only worked out what she had said to me as I ran in the bedroom when I had got my breath back and come to my senses. *What's that around your neck?* was going round and round in my head until I finally got up and looked in the mirror. A choker, a heavy gold chain with a snake, a gold snake with jewels encrusted into it, it has eyes—*Green Eyes.*

That night as I lay in bed I could hear chanting coming from the Temple. I pulled the blankets over my head to drown out the sound of the repetitive chant.

'Hum Ba Humba too
Find, find, find,
Betray, betray, betray,
Spy, spy, spy,
Hum Ba Humba too'

I shut my eyes. I could see Green lights—eyes—glowing eyes. The eyes on the snake around my neck started to glow, the chanting was getting louder and louder!

All you can see in my mirror at night is darkness, tonight—Two green lights!

There is a Temple up the road from us, I wish there wasn't.

The Ugly Rebel

This story was written by Kathryn for her mother Helen.

Not the right colour. Not the right size. Definitely not neat and tidy. Erica did not have colourful, glossy National Geographic style feathers like the other ducklings. Plain, uninviting grey stubble replaced the dark browns and glowing shades of red that should have painted her back. All the mother ducklings disowned her and cast her out of the polite society of the pond. They left her to aimlessly float amongst the less fashionable weeds in the bad end of the meadow.

Erica had no choice but to rebel. If she was not going to be blessed with the 'gorgeous' coloured feathers that the other ducklings had, then that was fine.

She decided she was an individual. So she turned to the well-known feather-dye brand Duckore, mixed it in a small pool and dived in. When Erica emerged, her grey stubble had magically turned into a greasy shade of jet black.

All the mother ducks shook their heads as Erica swam through the pond in her slick new feather-style. This was not enough. Erica needed something more something dramatic, something that would make sure that everyone knew that she didn't want to be accepted anyway.

What Erica needed was a *bill-ring*. Sammy the snake was kind enough to oblige. After one swift bite, Sammy had not only created a nice, neat hole but also installed a ring-pull that some careless person had dropped during a picnic. Erica thought they were sure to realise that she didn't give a damn what they thought now.

The mother ducks were outraged. They shook their heads, and gossiped among the reeds:

'What has she done now?'

'Always knew she was a bad egg that one.'

'My Charlie would never do a thing like that!'

'Such a shame.'

'Huh!' thought Erica. 'I'll show them I'll do whatever I want! Her "Charlie" is so damn wet, water wouldn't even slide off his back.' Erica needed to find something new, something different, something that had never been done before. So she decided to get a tattoo.

She paddled over to the reeds and asked Stevie the stick insect, if he would mind tattooing 'bite me' into her leg. He said he would be honoured. In no time at all, with Stevie and a little green dye made from the weeds, Erica had a highly original band tattoo around her little leg, just above her large, far from graceful, webbed foot.

The problem is, how often do you see a duck's foot. It spends so much time under water. In other words, no one noticed Erica's new tattoo. She was very disappointed and hid away in the reeds for a very long time. So long that the so-called permanent dye faded out of her feathers. So long that her bill grew and she had to remove her ring-pull-stud. So long that her scaly legs flaked away until her tattoo was gone.

Reluctantly Erica swam out from the reeds. She had been in there so long that the ducks living in the pond now had forgotten who she was, let alone how controversial her youth had been. One thing was still the same. People still muttered as she swam by. Not because of a bad feather-dye job, not because of a bit of commercial metal jutting out of her bill and not because she had 'bite me' scrawled around her leg. This time they muttered because she was, of course, a graceful swan.

Silence Tells All

Darkness filled the room. A thick blanket of silence made movement impossible. Deep breaths echoed. A door creaked. The walls began to laugh an eerie, evil laugh. An icy shiver ran up his spine as he turned around ... Louise slammed the book shut and wondered why she could never write anything like that.

Published in 'Youth Writes' Number 11 1999–2000, *An Anthology of Young Australian Writing*, page 119.

The Scramble for Love

Kathryn Carter aged 12
Winner of the PLC
Writer of the Year
Competition

We were squashed, packed in a truck. I was afraid. I felt a warm body pressing against mine. I introduced myself as we were going to be together for quite some time. His name was Peter. We talked for hours, and I must admit that I fell quite hopelessly in love with him. I later found out he felt the same way about me.

We were taken out of the truck and put in a huge room that was filled with other prisoners waiting to be sold.

Peter and I huddled together. We were frightened, terrified of being separated. I felt safe with Peter. It was a different kind of safe, different to any feeling of safety I had ever felt before. A lady bought us; Peter and another ten. Her name was Sarah. She took us to her home and flung us in a small room and slammed the door. It bounced and was still open a little bit, just enough to provide sufficient light. We had all been thrown about a bit, but no one was hurt. Suddenly I realized that I could not find Peter! An empty feeling filled my centre and it started turning over and over. A tear filled my eye and was followed by another. My sight was blurred but I could make out a familiar figure.

'Oh Peter, when I could not find you, I thought the worst!'

'It's alright Penny, I was only lost in the crowd. I am here now ... Penny!'

'Yes.'

'I am worried for your safety in this cruel world.'

'Oh Peter, sweet Peter. I will be safe while you are here to protect me. Oh, say you will look after me until the flame of fate is upon us.'

'I will, Penny, if you will be mine. I will take you through the scrambles of life, the great fire and beyond.'

1996

'Oh Peter, will you promise that I will always be the one and the only one for you, that I may be yours until the day that you are whole no more?'

'Penny?'

'Yes?'

'Sarah is cooking bacon tonight'

'That means ...?'

'Yes.'

'Oh Peter, we must escape.'

'Yes Penny, tonight we will enter the great beyond and escape the walls that have cartoned our love.'

'No Peter, we must go now while the coast is clear!'

'Yes, you are right.'

The two lovers escaped and started on their way to freedom.

They had nearly escaped when ...

'Oh Peter, the edge!'

But it was too late. Peter had fallen.

'Oh Peter, my dearest Peter, what a way to separate our love. You were so brave, to go against the dozen and now ... Oh Peter, my dearest Peter. Why? I ask why! God, why did you take my one and only love away from me? My life is no longer worth living. Take me too!'

At that moment Sarah came. She took away the remains of Peter and came back for Penny. She fulfilled Penny's wish of death. She had an omelette for dinner.

The Feather

Georgia walked down the pebbled street. She was supposed to go straight home from school but a man caught her eye. He was putting up a poster that read 'YOUR COUNTRY WANTS YOU!' On the poster was a man that was dressed in an army uniform with his finger pointing out. Georgia shrugged and kept on walking. When she got home her mother stood in the kitchen with a grave look on her face. Georgia asked her mother what was wrong. Her mother looked at the ground. Georgia was beginning to worry so she walked quickly into the living room. Her father sat in the big chair staring off into space. Georgia looked for a while and then spotted a white feather in his hand. Her father had decided not to enter the army because he wanted to look after his family. 'Don't worry, Father, what do they know!' Georgia asked her father trying to comfort him.

'They know I'm a coward that's what they know!' Georgia's father snapped back and then his hand went to his cheek 'A coward that's what I am.' He sat back in the armchair and a tear filled his eye. 'Get out of my sight!'

Georgia ran to her mother and threw her arms around her. 'Leave your father alone! He's very upset, those horrible people I bet it was those Johnsons next door. She's always boasting about her family, all her boys are going to fight and her husband!'

When Georgia woke up the next morning her father wasn't home. He started work in an hour from now but he was nowhere to be seen. Georgia ran into the kitchen, her white hair all over the place, to ask her mother where her father was. Her mother did not know. They spotted the white feather in the vase.

Soon he returned home and said 'We won't be needing this'. He picked up the feather out of the vase and threw it on the fire. Georgia's mother put her hand to her mouth and ran to her bedroom her eyes filled with tears. Georgia looked at her father and ran to her mother. Georgia's father Peter was left on his own. Soon Sam, his son, came in to him and said 'Father are you really going to fight? ... Yes ... OH ...that's fantastic.' He went off making gunshot noises and some unbearable bombing noises. He was fourteen but you would never know it to look at his behaviour.

He had signed up. Georgia was glad because she didn't want a coward as a father. Then her brother came into the room making those horrible noises. 'You're such a coward' Georgia said to her brother. 'You make those noises and think you're so smart but you're not brave, smart or anything!'

'I am so' replied her brother.

'Well why haven't you signed up?' Georgia teased.

'I'm too young' said her brother in defence of his pride.

'Haven't you heard of lying?' Georgia teased.

'Mother and Father wouldn't let me' Sam tried to convince his sister.

'Who's going to tell them' she replied.

'Where's Sam, Georgia?' asked Georgia's mother.

'I have no idea' lied Georgia with a smug look on her face.

'Yes you do' said her mother. She saw straight through the lie. 'Tell me!' she ordered her daughter.

'He's signed up' mumbled Georgia.

'Georgia speak up!' demanded her mother. 'You're not lying to me?' Georgia's mother just couldn't believe it.

'NO!' screamed Georgia and she ran out of the room.

'Goodbye honey' Georgia's father said to his wife before he kissed her goodbye.

'Do you have to go?' inquired Georgia's mother after the beloved kiss.

'Yes, but I will write!' Then Peter turned to his daughter and said 'Goodbye Princess!' and with that he picked Georgia up in his arms and she kissed him on the cheek. Soon the train pulled up and it was time for Georgia's father to go. Georgia's mother took out her white handkerchief, wiped her eyes and waved with it. Peter hung out the window to wave to his family. Although there was one missing. Sam. He had already gone to fight but they hadn't told Peter because they didn't want to worry him before he left. They lied to him and said he had to do some schoolwork! Georgia chased the train along the station next to the window where her father was. Once the train had pulled away Georgia ran back to her mother. There were tears in her mother's eyes but Georgia who didn't really understand the real meaning of war didn't think that anything would happen to her father.

Changing Attitudes

The Graceful Miss Whatkins smudged the red chalk in an attempt to rub it out. Her gold bracelets swayed, gently keeping a defiant beat. She turned and glared at the class, her eyes deeply concentrated on something else. The teacher tilted her head, scratched her neck and began to talk in her deep, bored, meaningless voice, 'Now class, for elderly-persons week our class—being the oldest—is going to help some elderly people with some day-to-day things'.

'Why bother? They're goin' to die soon, they're not goin' to worry if they go with a clean house or a mowed lawn!' cried Nigel Whip from the back of the room.

'Yeah! And they are all blind, so they aren't going to see any difference!' agreed Ruth Bartholomew who was sitting with her chair the wrong way round.

Then piped up Annie, 'I think that it is a lovely thing to do, those poor old dears—we have to feel sorry for them'.

Miss Whatkins turned to the teacher's pet and smiled at her with adoration. 'You will spend all tomorrow with them, helping. I will now read out the names and addresses of the elderly person that you will each have to look after'. The teacher started to read out the names of the *oldies* that each of the children would have to look after. The last name read out was 'Mrs Bennet'. She was handed to the care of a young girl that had remained quiet up until now, Elizabeth Michelle.

Everyone burst out 'Sucked in Lizzy!!!' and laughed at Lizzy. They all felt sorry for her. Mrs Bennet was a crazy purple-haired dreamer that lived in a world of her own! Lizzy groaned.

The next day was hot, the sun shone brightly. It was rather like the day that Australia was first bombed in World War 2. Lizzy was worried. The world was against her!

Mrs Bennet was also freaked out this psycho teenager was going to come and patronize her! 'The children of today, always trying to be polite and nice to the "Poor old *oldies*"! They are absolutely, horribly NICE! Anyway, what would the neighbours think? That I needed help? That the job of hanging out my undies was becoming too much?' thought Mrs Bennet and she took a long hard suck on her cigarette.

Soon the minute when the two totally different worlds would meet, possibly resulting in a terrible paradox, was upon the two, the geriatric and the rebellious teenager.

Lizzy finally reached the house and knocked on the red door, the sort of door that you have not seen since 1920. On the other side Mrs Bennet walked to the door still in a state of panic about the weirdo kid on the other side! Still, she opened the door and let the adolescent in and asked her name. 'Lizzy' she replied. *I wish you would drop dead!* was the thought going through her head. 'You're Mrs Bennet, aren't you?' shouted Lizzy.

'Yes' was the reply back but *Get lost you freak* was going through her head and she had to bite her tongue to stop herself from saying what she really thought towards the comment that had been made! 'Come in' said Mrs Bennet trying to sound hospitable to the over-polite guest. 'Would you like something to drink?' asked Mrs Bennet.

'Yes' said Lizzy and remembering that all *oldies* drank tea added 'Tea's fine thank you' .

'Right' said Mrs Bennet and went to work pottering around in the kitchen. Soon the kettle was serenading, telling the world that the tea was ready. Mrs Bennet poured the liquid into a china cup with buttercups painted delicately on it. Then, much to Lizzy's dismay, returned to the fridge and produced a can of coke, popped the lid and slurped up the fizzy drink.

When the silent morning tea had ended Mrs Bennet sent Lizzy off to mow the lawn, vacuum the house, polish the brass and to pull out the weeds from the garden. Lizzy finally completed the tasks that were given to her and entered the small house and approached the purple-haired *oldie*: 'I've finished' droned Lizzy and Mrs Bennet replied 'Good, now sit down and tell me something or other!' Mrs Bennet was trying her best to do as the bossy Miss Whatkins had ordered.

Lizzy sat down and thought about what she could give the *Poor old dear* to think about. Lizzy gave up and decided to wait for Mrs Bennet to say something.

What on earth is she going to bore me with? Mrs Bennet was puzzled and, in the end, realizing that the only thing that hadn't changed over the years was that kids go to school settled on the line 'How is school?'

'Good.' What else could Lizzy have said? Finally, Lizzy came to the conclusion that this day was not going too well and that neither of them was enjoying the company, so she said 'Look, I've finished the work and..., Well if you won't tell Miss Whatkins then I won't. I know you want rid of me from your house and I'm not getting out of it so let's call it a day!'

'Sure' said Mrs Bennet and showed Lizzy to the door. Lizzy did not hesitate to leave and was soon on her way and left Mrs Bennet thinking 'What a wonderfully horrible kid!'

Silence

Simon sat in the back seat of the Hover-Car. He listened to his parents arguing: 'Look, it's not my fault the food hydrator broke!' Simon's mother was trying to sound reasonable. 'Well it wasn't my fault!' Simon's father had given up trying to be reasonable long ago. The two grownups argued and argued. Simon's father took his hands off the wheel to explain to his wife what must have happened to the food hydrator. He was in the middle of his explanation when Simon's mother shouted out 'Look out!' Simon's eyes shot quickly across to see a cocker spaniel chasing a hover-bone across the road. The car swooped to miss the small dog but the 2096 Ford Lazer Floater swung, the brakes screeched there was a scream from the front seat and then—silence!

Come into My Parlour Said the Spider to the Fly

In a dark wood, in a dark country, in a particularly dark world a spider web glistened in a moonlight that did not seem to be shining. A black hairy creature sat in the middle and admired its work. Loops and flips, spins and circles, leaps and many interesting twists—all very complicated and yet all very essential—had come together to form a pretty good piece of work if the spider did say so himself. He felt awfully content as the night sky looked down on him, the trees brushed by him and several weak females feared him, not knowing their own strengths. All he was missing was prey. No sooner had he realized the incompleteness of the situation when a small creature buzzed by.

'Come into my parlour' said the spider to the fly. 'I have something I think you would like to see.'

'Really? How do you know what I want to see?' asked the fly who had just ended a rather serious relationship with a very messy break up and was sure that no one knew or understood her.

'Oh, I know everything. The world is at my command.'

'The world, maybe, but I am certainly not. I can see through any plot, scheme or trick and I never take orders.'

'I bet that I could outsmart you my dear. How are you at riddles?'

Stella and Kat

'I can solve the hardest riddle with my eyes closed, find the answer to the most difficult of questions, solve the unsolvable and make sense of the senseless.'

'Quite good then?' queried the spider who did not really understand a word that the fly had said, which is not a good sign. One of the greatest rules of riddles is that you must know more than your opponent. It is not fair otherwise.

'Fire away!' demanded the Fly.

'Why is a raven like a writing desk?'

'It isn't. That is just one of those ridiculous questions that people ask and call riddles when they can't think of anything to say. It is no more than a lame attempt to sound intelligent. It usually works as no one actually knows why a raven is like a writing desk—because it is not and so they give up thinking they are wrong. Why are you wasting my time?'

'Ah, shall I try another?'

'If you like, I have nothing better to do.'

'What came first the chicken or the egg?'

'That is not even a riddle. It is a silly question that foolish people spend their lives trying to solve simply for the sake of being able to call themselves philosophers.'

'True, you are more intelligent than I thought. I shall have to ask you a really good one ...'

'All right but try asking me an actual riddle—one with a solution this time.'

'If I do, and you can't solve it, will you promise to fly into my web? Let me show you my parlour?' After that the Spider attempted an evil laugh but it did not work and he felt foolish.

'Well that is the most ridiculous thing anyone has asked me to promise. I will see your parlour as you put it, if you can outsmart me that is and if you can answer my riddle.'

'Very well, it's a deal. Come and shake my hand.'

'I am not that gullible, besides, which one would I shake?'

'All right, are you ready?'

'Yes ... just get on with it.'

'When is a door not a door?'

'Tricky, I will give you credit for that. That does inspire thought—but not much I am afraid. A door is not a door when it is a jar.'

'Oh, well, you are a clever little insect aren't you. Go on and ask me your riddle. I think you will find I too am cleverer than you think.'

'All right, if a spider lives on a web, a flat surface made by thin twine, where is its parlour?'

Somewhere above, the moon and the stars really did shine. They looked down on the pair as they stared at each other in silence, both patiently waiting for the other to think of something to say, a riddle to ask—or heaven forbid—an answer to a really sensible question.

All a Bit Fishy …

Thomas tried to move his tail. He tried very hard, but with no success. He wasn't quite sure why, to begin with. After a bit more effort, in the hope that it was a passing fad, he discovered it was because he didn't have a tail. This presented a problem on a whole new level for Thomas. He couldn't remember ever not having a tail before. It's one of those things he was sure he wouldn't forget. In fact, he was quite sure that he was (or at the very least had been) a goldfish, and lacking a tail was a fairly major personality crisis for him.

After this shocking revelation, in quick succession, came the discoveries that he wasn't swimming in water and that he was very similar to a human. So similar to a human that the casual observer would have mistaken Thomas for any other ordinary person. The only thing stopping Thomas from actually being human was his absolute conviction that he was fundamentally a goldfish. Admittedly, he could only remember about three seconds of being a goldfish, but that constituted his entire existence before these rather rude discoveries. And to be quite frank, he missed having gills.

He spent a moment or three examining his surroundings. A plain room, with a door, another door leading to a balcony and another door that was actually a window. There were no more doors, but of course there was the bed he was lying on and a fish tank on a table beside it. He was quite pleased with himself. He'd never really examined anything before, on account of being a goldfish. It had been quite unnecessary, and coupled with a three-second memory, quite useless. So he revelled in the use of a new faculty. He paused for a moment. 'If I was really a goldfish, and goldfish can't remember things, then now, not (seemingly) being a goldfish, and therefore remembering things, am I still me?' Of course this led to an entirely new conundrum, being that if he had always been a goldfish, and had only recently managed to become a human, how was he managing to think in an English vocabulary.

He stood up and fell over. Actually, that's a lie. It's very difficult to describe in words what he did do. He certainly fell over. But the standing up and falling over weren't really different things. It wasn't a human 'Here I am with my centre of gravity two feet above where it was before I initiated this complicated manoeuvre, now where are my legs aarrghh', type of standing up then falling over. The whole concept of a centre of gravity was completely new to Thomas. This wasn't particularly pleasant for the former fish. Rather, he tried to stand up horizontally a metre above the floor without using his arms or legs. Certainly arms and legs became involved, but the same casual observer we met before probably would have either called an ambulance or applauded as if it were a particularly good busking performance.

The specific casual observer we are talking about applauded. He had, at some point, miraculously appeared where the door was, along with some blank space and a degree of another room. The door, in turn, had moved its width along the wall and turned its back to Thomas, who was quite impressed with the display and applauded back. The door didn't respond, so Thomas, in a respectful manner, stood on the bed, attempted to lever himself to the ceiling by use of the empty light fitting and began to lick it.

At this point someone else entered the room. 'What' the doctor inquired, 'are you doing?' Thomas continued to lick the ceiling. After a considerable pause, in which the only sound was the slight 'lap lap lap' of Thomas' tongue, he lowered himself back down onto the bed. It only then occurred to him that he had in the past few minutes demonstrated the full proper use of his new body. He looked at it suspiciously, like a sushimi chef would look at a scotsman with a frying pan and a lemon trying to hide something behind his back. The doctor, however, merely repeated his question.

'Well, it's only manners, isn't it!' said Thomas, recovering himself as he collapsed more comfortably onto the floor. The doctor looked at him quizzically. 'Isn't it?' The doctor still seemed unsatisfied. Thomas took his mind back to the far-off darkling days of water and plastic divers, and dragged his knowledge from what he could only describe as racial memory.

With a reverent pause, he continued to explain what was as close to religion goldfish got. 'It is a basic precept of life, handed down from time immemorial, that there is a close link between food and humans. A human walks in, and then the food floats down from the ceiling ... I thought everyone knew that ...' The serious expression on Thomas' face conveyed the deep import and significance of his message.

The first man applauded again, for no apparent reason, an effect exacerbated by the fact that he was now in between the door and the wall. 'You'll have to excuse him,' explained the doctor. 'He's our resident madman.' The person in question demonstrated this ably by tentatively asking the door to join him in singing a round of 'We wish you a merry Christmas.' Although Thomas, until very recently, had been a goldfish, and therefore had many questions, he felt obliged to ask why it was that they (whoever they might be) had a resident madman. Calmly, the doctor responded 'Because we couldn't find one that would come in for part time work.'

Thomas rather felt that he was missing the point, but as this was his first attempt at being human, he thought he'd leave the finer points of skill up to the experts. Instead, he got straight to the point: 'Why am I not a goldfish? I'm quite sure I was a goldfish this morning. I'm almost certain that I could inhale water at lunchtime. Even right up until this afternoon, I quite distinctly recollect being a goldfish. Why is it that now I have to contend with strange things like legs and centres of gravity?'

The doctor looked sternly across his steel-rimmed spectacles at Thomas, and frowned. 'Thomas, I regret to inform you, that I believe you are not, will not be, and furthermore, never have been a goldfish. If you were, as you claim, how could you remember what you were this morning, or at lunchtime, or this afternoon? It's a well-known fact that goldfish only have a three-second memory. To be quite frank, I've no idea what you are or where you came from. Or even, come to think of it, myself. I must have a degree from somewhere, because I am The Doctor, but I can't remember where. As far as my present knowledge extends, we could both be entirely fictional characters.' Thomas, deciding that, for the moment, metaphysics should remain in the realm of science fiction, attempted to soothe the doctor as he would any ailing friend and blew bubbles at the confused man. Unfortunately, it merely led to some threads of dribble to forlornly spread across a bare patch of floor, but surely it's the thought that counts.

In the background, the door boomed out the bass tones of Christmas carols to the accompaniment of the resident madman, who was used to this sort of thing, but had a rather reedy voice.

SPEECHES

Seeds of Success

Every person is a seed with the possibility of success, but it is the nurturing of the seed that often decides whether the seed will in fact be successful and blossom into a healthy well-nurtured plant. Where does this nurturing come from? A lot is given at home but some of the most important types of nurturing, the experiences, with other people your own age, can only come at Kindergarten.

Kindergarten is derived from the German word Kindergarten which, when translated, means Kinder-Child and Garten-Garden—so it is 'Garden for children'. Obviously reflecting the nurturing and basic sense of morality that you gain at Kindergarten. Because all you really need to know to succeed in life is not there in the piece of paper you receive when you graduate from University but is there in the sand pit at Kindergarten.

Just think of all the experiences that you obtain at Kindergarten.

I remember pushing and shoving to get to the front of the line for orange juice. The order had been decided and I had managed to push my way to be first—first to get my orange juice when the teacher reversed the order.

I spent hours building the best tower of blocks that had ever made its way onto the playmat when one of my classmates knocked it over in a matter of seconds when I turned my head to get another blue block.

I had finger-painted the masterpiece of the century, the modern Mona Lisa! Then the teacher washed it off.

It was my birthday, and I had a cake, but the teacher told me that everyone had to have some too.

1997

Simple lessons that appear to bear no relevance after Kindergarten? Look at the hidden messages.

You will never succeed and win with violence.

Destruction is faster than creation and nothing will last forever so look after it while you have it.

That all the fun and advantages come in the doing not the final product.

And that sharing is important, other people have feelings and everyone likes cake.

So, although these messages may be added to after Kindergarten they are planted you may say in Kindergarten.

Kindergarten promotes a lot of hope, it lets you have a vision that can be as broad and amazing as your imagination will let you. You are encouraged to have goals and visions at Kindergarten. At my Kindergarten there was one boy, Paul, who was quite shy; he hardly spoke a word until one day he went outside, stuck his head between the railings and got stuck there. The teacher, trying not to laugh, quickly rang 000 to summon the fire brigade. But it wasn't just the fire brigade that came, we had: the rescue squad, the police, the ambulance, as well as the fire brigade all in the serenading trucks and vans and all to rescue poor little Paul who had now become quite a celebrity with his classmates. He loved it. He was the centre of attention. Once he had been cut out of the bars his speech improved and he developed quite an ambition to become a fireman.

Kindergarten is perfect work experience.

Success is to be a healthy well-nurtured plant, but plants need to be situated in the right conditions and they need to be happy in their surroundings because otherwise they will wilt and die. We are like plants; if our surroundings are not right, we are not happy; we don't go as extreme as plants and die but we will not be reaching our capable standard. In today's society people generally spend a lot of time at work and so we need to be happy.

KINDERGARTEN IS THE PERFECT WORK EXPERIENCE:

In Kindergarten I was: a nurse, a doctor, a princess, a lion, an alien, a ballerina, a witch, a mother and even a father with no qualifications or obligations. These opportunities don't come as easily anywhere else.

Just think of the budding artists finger painting.

All the soon-to-be builders playing with blocks.

All the budding politicians organising who else is going to tidy what.

And all the gymnasts or escapees playing on the climbing equipment.

All getting a taste of what they might do in later years.

When you are young and you are at Kindergarten you have no pre-conceptions, you are very tolerant. Everyone is the same and you don't judge people on their colour or culture. This is mainly due to the fact that no such judgment has been imposed on you and Kindergarten continues to maintain this tolerance. It encourages you to see people as they are and not what colour they are or where they come from. And at Kindergarten you are exposed to a lot of different cultures and people. You come in contact with children who are black, white or somewhere in-between. Children with Downs syndrome or Cerebral Palsy—there was one boy at my Kindergarten who had such severe Cerebral Palsy he could not walk. I didn't think any less of him. I really didn't notice that he was that different.

Because my Kindergarten told me that he was in fact just like me and he really wasn't different. You also come into contact with people who are slow learners because there are no separate classes at Kindergarten like there are in later school years. You meet people who can't speak much English. People who can't speak any English and sometimes even people who can't speak at all. All these people are working together in harmony not worrying about what everyone looks like or where they come from.

I remember my final Christmas concert at Kindergarten. There we stood around the piano: 3 Marys—one of which was male, 3 Josephs, 16 Wisemen and an uncountable number of sheep all standing together. All the Dandelions, Roses and Sunflowers standing together and all reaching for the same sun. All holding with them the basic morals they need to know in life. To play fair, to be kind, sharing is important, milk, cookies and a sleep in the afternoon are good for you and much more. All seedlings that had been nurtured and hold every possibility of success.

At the Cross-Roads

There is an old story:

It was a dark night. The only light was the reflection of the moon on the snow that was falling quite heavily. A doctor lazed around his surgery enjoying the warmth of an open fire when he received a message. A mother was in labour but there was some difficulty, and the mother and the child's life were in danger. Now this particular mother lived way out in the country, and it was quite a distance to travel to get to her—especially in the snow.

He was faced with a sort of cross-roads or a choice. He could go one way and try to save the child's life but most probably kill himself on the way. Or he could take the other path and save his life but then the child would most probably die.

When all we can see is the choice, the ideas or possible decisions, we cannot see right or wrong or good or bad. This is because there is no such thing as good or bad choices or decisions, just good and bad consequences. There is no such thing as a good or bad road; it all depends on what you do on the way. At the cross-roads you cannot choose a wrong path.

Many new plants and animals have been discovered and choice has been made to bring them back to the main cities to be studied and often eventually used. This is often to our advantage because where would we be without the potato or Quinine which cures malaria, but other substances are not so good. Sir Frances Drake discovered Tobacco—he thought he had made a great discovery when he brought it back to England, just as Sir Walter Raleigh thought he was very clever when he discovered you could smoke it. Now these discoveries or choices have obviously resulted in bad consequences as millions of people cough their way closer to death each day. In the words of John Lennon 'and curse

Sir Walter Raleigh he was such a stupid git'. But is it such a bad choice to make a new discovery and to bring it back to your home to be studied? I mean is it such a bad decision to find a use for a discovery. You see it is all in the way that you use your choices—the choices or decisions themselves are not good or bad.

About 16 years ago a dog strolled into my mother's pre-school. He had no tag, collar or any identification. My mother took him to the pound, but no one claimed him. My parents decided to keep him while they found him a 'suitable home'. Six months later he was still living with them. My mother received a phone call one day from my father that simply stated, 'YOUR DOG IS GOING!' My mother came tearing home to find the dog, now named Harvey, hiding in the laundry, my father's wallet destroyed, partly eaten money floating around the garden and a few bits of credit card being pecked at by a bird. My father had now decided the consequences of this good decision had been BAD (but) he still chose to forgive him for the wallet incident. My father has decided that this had good consequences as it later became—Dad comes home from work: Hi Kathryn, Hi Helen— HARVEY!!!!

In today's society an awful lot has become a cliché through over-use. Just think of all the movies that have been released in the last couple of years: *Casper, James Bond, Mission*

Impossible, Hamlet, Romeo and Juliet, The Addams family and *Lost in Space. The Man in the Iron Mask* has been made and remade at least five times and yet people still wonder why the critics are saying it is stale. You see a very common trait is for people to choose a route that is familiar as the familiar is safe. It is obviously believed by many movie producers that to tread on a path that is well and truly worn is safer than to do something completely different.

One of the greatest tragedies of all time has become one of the greatest cliches of all time. *The Titanic* or some aspect of the Titanic has made it into a film at least three times and everyone has used it in a public speech. OK, we know it sank.

Everyone seems to know the Titanic sank, it is one of those inevitable facts that hits everyone in the face. Despite the monotony of this story the movie producers today seem to think that with a lot of over marketing and a blond American they can sell anything. The scary thing is they seem to be right. This worn track by the producer of the latest *Titanic* movie has overtaken *Star Wars* to have the biggest selling movie. It is estimated that *Godzilla*, another remake of a remake, is going to outsell *Titanic* on a similarly worn path.

A lot of cross-roads appear to have a good choice of paths and yet this can be very misleading as it all depends very much on what happens along the way.

When faced with the choice of taking your life, dying, or keeping your life, life would seem to be a path to take at the cross-roads. There is a man, an American author, Robert Fulghum, who at one stage in his life chose death. But his problems or choices did not end there. He was faced by the decision of how to kill himself; after flying to Mexico the idea of buying a gun seemed the best option. This seemed the best path but when he found there was a waiting period for a gun, he changed his mind. Next, he decided to throw himself off a building or some great height. But in this part of Mexico there were no particularly high points. Then of course there was the mess factor—he didn't really want someone to clean him off the footpath, so he decided to drive into the desert and fix a hose to his exhaust and depart that way. However, the hose he bought was round and the exhaust was oval, so he was faced with 'how to join it?' He eventually used tape desperately trying to bridge the gap between the oval and the circle. He finally managed to attach the tape and the hose fell off. He ended up laughing at himself at his own inability—he realised that, in his words, 'what he wanted wasn't death but more life' (Robert Fulghum). The consequence of his choice at the cross-roads was good. He discovered life once again although from the initial outlook of the path you would have said the consequences would be bad.

That doctor chose to leave the warmth of his fire and set out into that cold night. He made his way through the snow and he eventually reached the distressed mother. The doctor secured the birth, the mother and child survived. Mr and Mrs Hitler were very grateful, and they said so as they gazed at their child, which they named Adolf.

Many people believe that if we study the road and all the factors involved closely then we can avoid these bad consequences, but I ask you this: would you choose the path that would turn away from a dying baby just in case?

Fool's Paradise

Our world is, always has been and always will be a fool's paradise. We encourage people to be foolish, we deal with things in a basically foolish way and time after time we simply are generally foolish.

Not only that but one of the things that unites almost the whole world is foolish ideas. I mean Saturday April the tenth was the day to get lucky if you wanted a baby for the turn of the millennium or if you wanted a million dollars for that matter. On this date all over the world competitions promising up to and over a million dollars were being offered to the couple that has the pleasure of writing themselves into the history books by having the first baby of the millennium. Family planning experts were in a state of panic, not about the millennium bug but about the millennium baby. In Britain, the family planning association has gone so far that they have plastered 'A baby is for life, not just for the millennium' on billboards all over the country. The thought that the fact human life must be considered as more than just a gimmick has to be pointed out to people in writing several metres tall is terrifying. But unfortunately, considering the fact that we seem to encourage foolish behaviour and ideas to such a mammoth degree, it is sadly necessary.

On the 27th of October this year a blue cow was found at Circular Quay. Now putting aside the fact that someone dumping a full-sized cow that was not only decomposing but also painted bright blue is ongoing proof of all the eccentric fools Australia plays host to, it also demonstrated how foolish we are when it comes to dealing with things that are out of the ordinary. You see the problem was that no one wanted to take responsibility for the cow. The museum of contemporary art dis-owned it, a local contemporary artist—Jason Rogers—said he had a great deal of respect for the cow but it wasn't his; the police said it may as well have fallen out of the sky. The reason the police were so keen to find who was responsible for the cow—which had the label 'for everyone who has struggled for an answer, Brad'—was so they knew who to fine. Yes, you see this cow, which has since been burnt, has been classified as a very large bit of litter. One would hope that it was the origins of the cow that were important to the fools that govern our country but that is asking too much when there is the possibility of a fine.

The biggest problem is that it seems that it is not just people in authority that are foolish. People in general are, on an everyday level, already indoctrinated into the ways of the foolish. In column 8 of the *Sydney Morning Herald* was reported that a man was seen in the maternity ward of a hospital comforting a newly born baby not by singing to it but by playing it one of the tunes that was programmed into his mobile phone. I ask you how on earth is the organised high-pitched beeping of a mobile phone supposed to comfort a child? It can't. It is as simple as that. It is just foolish. But then again people are steadily becoming more and more foolish. Now if you buy a blowtorch it displays the warning: Do not use as a hair dryer. If you buy deodorant it says: Do not spray over food and if you buy a chain saw you will find the warning: Do not stop with your hands.

I mean after all who would have to go down as being one of the biggest fools in the history of the planet but instead is remembered as a hero? Christopher Columbus. You see Columbus was going along on his way, hoping to find a better shipping route to India, took a wrong turn and ended up landing smack bang into America. Because of this mistake this historical fool never found a better route to India—but hey, thanks to him we have America. Is he outcast as that fool who got lost on a route that had been travelled by many before him? No. Is he remembered as the idiot who couldn't follow a map? No. Despite the fact he took a major wrong turn he is hailed as one of the best explorers of all time. Our world is simply a garden of Eden for the foolish, a place where their stupidity is hailed as an achievement.

So what can we do? Our planet is plagued with fools. People who declare war on each other when peace is not completely out of the question, people who are obsessed with the wording of what could be a very simple question and people who just can't get over all the different rings they can program into their mobile phone. But when it comes down to it, we are kind of stuck with it. So we may as well sit back and enjoy the foolishness that surrounds us. Because, after all, our world is, always has been and always will be a fool's paradise.

Monique McDonald (fellow competitor)
Her year 12 jersey was appropriately titled 'drama queen' and when she spoke in the Voice of Youth I always admired how she had the ability to take you out of your own world and into the one she spoke of—a true story teller— the best kind of public speaker.

Barrie Fitz-Henry (Past President NSW Rostrum)
Her speeches were testimony to her passion for life and commitment to a job well done. Whether Kathryn was the victor or whether the prize eluded her, she was always gracious and friendly.

Greg McKay (National Co-ordinator—Rostrum Voice of Youth)
In her life Kathryn touched the lives of everyone she came into contact with. She showed by example how we should approach life—with enthusiasm and energy.

A Tribute to Kathryn Carter (1983–2003) *Rostrum Voice of Youth*

Against All Odds

Few can succeed against all odds in real life. In the movies Indiana Jones reaches the treasure in the nick of time against odds that have theatre goers glued to their seats. In the movies the treasure is clear immense wealth or the saving of a nation. In real life these sorts of treasures are out of reach for most of us. But for many the odds are against them from the beginning and their treasure can be as basic as a happy productive life.

A child is born, a new beginning. The odds of a child being born with Down Syndrome are not high but it does happen to many families. I know of a family who were sent a sympathy card at the birth of their child. This child, this family, has already had the odds out of their favour. Friends are reserved in their congratulations, families look for answers: 'Nothing like that on our side of the family'. Against all odds.

A child with Down Syndrome can have many other problems related with the syndrome. These can be severe and life threatening like heart disorders or as mild as a proneness to colds. Against all odds.

But against all odds these children grow and laugh and cry like all children. Today these children can go to school and be given the opportunities that they were once denied because they were different. The odds were against it but people realised that these children had the potential to develop as all children do. People, like parents, began to fight against the odds to make authorities realise that their children could learn and have a better quality of life. It was once said that Down's babies were so wonderfully placid and happy they were left to sleep. Now it is realised that with stimulation these babies can develop. Against all odds!

People with Down Syndrome have got quite flat skulls, and they do look slightly different. Because of this often people stare. Imagine what it would be like if every time you went anywhere people stared at you, stopped and looked. This is a massive obstacle to overcome—to have strong enough willpower to hold your head high and ignore the people around you. To fight against all odds.

My mother used to teach a class which was made up of mainly children with Down Syndrome. They would go for walks down to the pond in a nearby park to feed the ducks. In order to complete this journey there were a number of obstacles to overcome: the busy roads, the people shopping and the people staring. When the journey was complete and they had made it to the park [and defeated all odds], there would be no bread left.

I had a friend at pre-school who had Down Syndrome called Sarah. Finding her daughter a pre-school in the first place was extremely hard for Sarah's mother, but against all odds she found my pre-school. The only thing different about Sarah that I noticed was that she had a runnier nose to most people. This was probably due to her having small sinus tubes, and that she had a fascination with eating green playdough, she liked it even more than me! The reason for me not noticing any real difference is that really there are no major differences. People with Down Syndrome are just people. But they have to fight to show people that that is in fact the case. Children with Down Syndrome are just children. We have a friend who is a lecturer in America who has a seven-year-old son who has Down Syndrome. A couple of years ago they came out to visit us. The little boy—Peter— was no different to any other child, He laughed, he ran around, he talked, he had fun, he got tired, he got grumpy, he begged for a carry which anyone who has ever had any experience with children will tell you is the normal procedure for a tired child who has had enough. Peter like all children knew what he liked. He liked ice cream, but not just any ice cream, vanilla ice cream, and not just any vanilla ice cream, vanilla ice cream in a dish and the dish was essential. Like any child of his age to get what he wanted, the ice cream, Peter would do anything, go anywhere and say anything no matter how embarrassing, no matter how dangerous, or just plain heart bracingly pathetic to get it, in the end, against all odds he got his ice cream. We took the 7-year-old boy around Sydney, we went to the aquarium, explored Darling Harbour and came here—the National Maritime Museum. We were hoping to see the pirate show but we were too late. We looked at the displays then we came into this theatre, just to make sure it wasn't on. Peter would not leave the theatre! Mum sent me out in hope that he would follow my example and leave. After a while and no sign of Peter I returned to the theatre to find my mother in a trance as she watched the little boy giving a lecture to the empty room. We went down to the front and watched. Peter's speech wasn't very good and what he was saying was a mystery but every now and then words that he had picked up from his father lecturing and his teacher shone through like: *Sit down, Be quiet and thank you very much.* At the conclusion of his lesson Peter came up to my mother and I, thanked us for coming and shook our hands. He then confidently walked out of the room. In my eyes he had succeeded against all odds as he had given a very confident lecture.

So, like the hero in an adventure story, a person with Down Syndrome must fight against all odds, cross all boundaries in order to succeed and win the battle. However, the hero in an adventure story is not real and can give up at any time but a person with Down Syndrome is real, is fighting for their life, freedom and happiness. Fighting against all odds.

The Touch of Midas

Two boys were fighting in a school playground. As they tumbled around one boy wanted to win more than anything else. Finally, he pinned the other boy down. The boy on the hard cement shouted for mercy. As the apparent loser got up, he saw the other boy smile and so he said, 'If I lived in a house like yours and ate food like you eat, then I could have beaten you'. The winner got his wish but felt awful. He realised the whole fight was a big mistake.

Now everyone knows the story of the greedy ancient Greek King Midas. He was granted a wish and so he asked for the touch of gold. He really just wanted to gain even more wealth—he thought he would with this golden touch. As I am sure you all know, as far as choosing a good wish goes, Midas failed. Problems were evident when he tried to eat. Things proved worse when he tried to ride a horse. The thing that really got him was when he gave his daughter a nice big hug. Hungry and alone Midas began to admire the poorest beggars of his kingdom—they at least *could* eat. He was very disappointed as he realised his wish was no more than a curse. He was stuck in a hole of adversity. So, Midas asked to have his gift removed. He realised that he had made a mistake. His gift was removed. From then on Midas knew how to love and live in an unselfish way. So, I guess Midas did become wealthy—in an emotional sense rather than in a material sense. So often what we set out to achieve—but fail, is not nearly as good as what we achieve in the end. Problems often bring about the best results. We only have to look at Midas who encountered Failure, Disappointment, Adversity and mistakes but found the value of love. This idea of problems bringing the best results extends far beyond Greek mythology. Everyone comes face to face with problems and just like Midas it very often leads to reward or even success.

What is the greatest thing of all time that came about because of a failure? America. Yes, you see when Christopher Columbus discovered America, he was actually looking to find fame and fortune by finding a better shipping route to Asia. He never intended to discover a country. Naturally finding a country brings more reward than finding a shipping route and yet, technically, Christopher failed. He didn't find a better shipping route but the rewards from this failure were far better. Even failure can lead to achievement.

The sting of disappointment hits very hard but it too can lead to success. I knew a little girl in England who learnt ballet and let's be fair, she was pretty ... hopeless. Her class was performing a variation of Swan Lake. She wanted more than anything to be a Swan, but when parts were announced she was a **weed.** She was heartbroken. All she had to do was stand there and sway. The concert came, the piece was a complete failure. All the swans fell over in a sort of domino effect. At the end—the weed was the only one left standing. The audience applauded, slowly. Then one man stood up and yelled—'Let's hear it for the weed!' The whole audience got up and began to scream and shout and clap—she stole the show, quite an achievement seeing all she set out to achieve was to be a swan. Even disappointment can lead to success.

I personally experienced adversity at the beginning of this year. My debating team and I had prepared a fantastic debate. The debate was going to be a breeze. We got to the debate and discovered we had prepared the wrong side. Our first speaker bowed out, crying because we only had 25 minutes to prepare the entire debate. I was third speaker; I was halfway through my rebuttal, and I couldn't remember what side we were on. OK I told myself. I would hate to think what I did to the audience. The debate was a complete failure. But we won. Not only that but that was the one and only debate we won in that entire competition. Adversity really can lead to success.

Thomas Edison was a very intelligent man and yet he made over 2000 mistakes before he invented the light bulb. A reporter asked him how it felt to fail so many times. Edison replied 'I never failed once. I invented the Light Bulb. It just happened to be a 2000 step process'. In other words—those 2000 mistakes were not a waste of time. By making those mistakes he learnt what was wrong and finally found what was right. Mistakes are the best teachers.

You see problems often bring the best results.

The defeated boy's words echoed in the winner's head as he walked home. He thought how unfair it was that he should have more than enough and others not nearly enough. That boy was Albert Schweitzer. In 1931 he became a medical missionary in Africa. From that fight—that mistake—he learnt to care for people.

So next time something goes wrong think of Columbus who failed, the disappointed ballet dancing weed, my debating team who faced adversity, Thomas Edison who made over 2000 mistakes, and Albert Schweitzer. And of course, don't forget Midas who found the reward of love by failing by facing disappointment, by landing headfirst in adversity and by making a mistake. Because if you learn from your mistakes and let them lead you to success you will turn everything into gold and that is the true touch of Midas.

Where For Art Thou?

In Year 8 we studied *Romeo and Juliet*. Like every other person who has ever been faced with an essay on anything Shakespearean I ran helplessly to *Cliff's Notes* in the vain hope that they would translate what I was supposed to be studying. Whilst flipping through this paperback lifesaver I found a very interesting fact, 'Where for art thou Romeo?' does not mean *Where are you Romeo* rather it means *Why are you Romeo*?

Words play such a large part in our lives. Whole phrases can have a reputation. I mean *Where for art thou* is renowned as a cry for someone's true love. Now this great emphasis can be a problem as very often people get words wrong or misunderstand them completely. I mean how many people simply don't know the true meaning of *Where for art thou*. Today, words and numbers say and imply so much more than their literal meaning. That is why I feel a sense of horror every time I see that the school phone number ends in 666. All these implications and double meanings can be a problem as so often we get words wrong or simply misunderstand them completely.

Now due to the fact that I simply can't spell, I am completely reliant on my computer spell check. Sometimes I think it is like the blind leading the blind. For example, did you know that Barbie is in my computer's spell check? Although it keeps wanting to replace Howard with Coward, Keating with Cheating. The Klu Klux Klan is in there, but Greenpeace is not. Leonardo Da Vinci is a complete mystery to my computer spell check, but Christopher Columbus and God are fine as long as they are spelt with a capital. It is amazing what a steady influence America and Americanisations have on our language. The country that coined the word 'whatever' and brought us 'Go Ricky'. But do we really want to lose sight of our English language? Words like thou and art and doattee (which means to nod the head when sleep comes on whilst one is sitting up!).

However, do we really want to add even more words to our incredibly huge language considering just how wrong people manage to get not only words but phrases. Other than the infamous Where *for art thou Romeo?* Other big mistakes include the fact that Sherlock Holmes never said *Elementary my dear Watson,* Frankenstein is the creator not the monster and Captain Kirk never said *Beam me up Scotty!*

To make the English language even more confusing, we have had the one set of the feminist approach of *now we have burnt our bra now let's turn on the dictionary.* All words are being forced into non-gender specific forms. Now this would be fine, I mean some people do feel offended by how they are described, but it is getting out of hand. Today people are paranoid about their choice of words, to the degree where it is socially compulsory to blush as you say *human.*

But the truth of the matter is, *man* is not actually gender specific at all. It comes from the old English *mann* spelt with a double n, and means people. People in general. So in other words, all those raving feminists who refuse to be part of *Mankind* are simply saying that they are not people at all.

So, I have come to the conclusion that you should remember words are just words—and if they are going to bother you, then you should look them up and find out their true meaning. Perhaps if we all thought about what we are saying, what we are implying, and who we are quoting then maybe we would make fewer mistakes.

And by the way, next time you are feeling depressed about the fact that you have to write an essay on something Shakespearean and don't seem to understand a single word of it, take heart in the fact that in 400 years time, someone will be studying *10 Things I Hate About You* and will hear 'The difference between like and love is that I like my *Sketches,* but I love my *Prada backpack*' and they too will need to buy *Cliff Notes* in the vain hope that they will translate what they are supposed to be studying.

The Rhythm of Life

When a child is born, the very first thing that it will respond to is a smiling face. It doesn't even have to be a real face, a newly born child will even respond to a cardboard picture as long as it is happy.

'The rhythm of life, it's a powerful beat, puts a tingle in your fingers and a tingle in your feet, rhythm in the bedroom, rhythm in the street, yes the rhythm of life is a powerful beat.'

The Rhythm of Life. Who could forget this showstopper number from, what is personally my favourite musical, *Sweet Charity.* The Broadway sensation that also brought us *If my friends could see me now* and that all-time classic *Hey Big Spender.* But did you know that *The Rhythm of Life* was originally <u>not</u> in *Sweet Charity* at all? It was in fact added to the musical at the last minute. The musical director Cy Coleman decided that there was a certain something missing, something bright, something cheerful, something happy and something hopeful and so *The Rhythm of Life* was written into the script. Now isn't this something that we can all relate to? From when we are born, we are constantly looking for happy smiles and cheerful moments. It is because we, as people, all need bright, cheerful, happy and hopeful moments to drown out all the boredom, pain and loneliness that surrounds us. I call this *The Rhythm of Life* philosophy. It simply is, adding something that is pure happiness into something that desperately needs it. I mean, haven't we all been bored to death in a shopping centre and suddenly decided to serenade the whole place with our own variation of whatever is on the radio at that point in time? Of course! I often follow *The Rhythm of Life* philosophy myself, usually sometime during double maths, much to my teacher's dismay. Taking a moment to simply be happy is something that we all need to do sometime in one way or another. After all, it is a proven scientific fact that optimistic people live longer than pessimistic people do.

This was highlighted a couple of years ago when huge amounts of people, every morning, would queue up for one toll booth on the Sydney Harbour Bridge. When asked why, one motorist said: 'The lady who works there is just so friendly, her smile makes a nice start to a hard day at work.' In other words, these people had realized the true wonder of *The Rhythm of Life* philosophy that they would queue up for double the amount of time every morning just to experience it.

A boost of happiness can bring strength. For the elderly and the disabled life can become hard, lonely and definitely in need of some brightening up. Companion dogs, which can be found in hospitals and homes for the elderly, are carrying out *The Rhythm of Life* philosophy on a daily basis. An example of this, which is close to home for me, is my uncle who works in a retirement home. One day he took his dog, Sally, in for a visit. There was one particular man there who was almost catatonic; meaning he was in a state similar to that of a coma; when Sally approached him, he looked up, reached down and stroked her. And then he smiled. Companion dogs add something bright and cheerful into what could be quite a drab setting—no matter what the wallpaper, a hospital is still a hospital. You see there comes a time when we all find that our lives are flat and in need of some brightening up—we need to follow *The Rhythm of Life* philosophy and introduce a burst of happiness which can lead to a boost of self-esteem.

The Rhythm of Life philosophy can be very powerful. It can be so powerful that it can penetrate hate and war. In 1914, the world was divided by war. One place where you would think that the division would be far too immense to ever be reconciled would have been at the front line. However, in the Christmas of that year there was a cease-fire and the Germans and the British pulled themselves out of the mud, climbed out of their trenches and ran out onto the field and together they played ... soccer. They had both had enough of the pain and war that surrounded them. They both needed a burst of happiness. So, they followed *The Rhythm of Life* philosophy and together they enjoyed that moment of pure, hopeful happiness.

The Rhythm of Life philosophy can be applied anytime anywhere, no matter how desperate a situation may seem. In the *New York Times* magazine, July 1992, appeared a photo of a middle-aged man by the name of Vedran Smailovic. He was sitting on a café chair, wearing a tuxedo outside a bakery where Mortar fire killed 22 people waiting in line for bread in late May. Not only is he sitting in this precarious position, but he is playing the cello. He is a member of the Sarajevo Opera Orchestra.

He is a musician. There is very little he can do about hate and war, it has been going on in Sarajevo for centuries. So he simply follows T*he Rhythm of Life* philosophy and every day sits near that bakery and plays an Adagio in G minor. He may not be playing a showstopper number, but he is certainly bringing happiness and hope to the people around him. Almost everyone in Sarajevo knows that Cellist that sat outside the Bakery. In fact, the place where his Café chair sat has become a sort of casual shrine, a place of honour that Croats, Serbs, Muslims and Christians all know about. But it is not just in Sarajevo that the cellist is known; his simple story was published in the paper, an artist in Seattle saw his picture and read his story. She in turn organized a commemorative concert.

The true beauty of *The Rhythm of Life* is that it is such a well-known song, a song that many can sing along to. T*he Rhythm of Life* philosophy, of bringing happiness into a situation that needs it, can also be shared by many. This is shown by Vedran Smailovic and that artist in Seattle. You see one bright and happy act can inspire another. Who knows, if everyone followed *The Rhythm of Life* philosophy then perhaps we could have the whole world singing. After all, a small harmless puppy has the power to change a person from being sad to happy, happiness can be so powerful that people will queue up for a very long time for it. A simple, yet enjoyable game of soccer can unite even the strongest enemies and one cellist can penetrate the boundaries of war.

So, ladies and gentlemen, never forget:

'The rhythm of life, it's a powerful beat, puts a tingle in your fingers and a tingle in your feet, rhythm in the bedroom, rhythm in the street, yes the rhythm of life is a powerful beat.'

So, take advantage of it, follow *The Rhythm of Life* philosophy, and write a bright, cheerful, happy, hopeful showstopper number into your life.

If Only They Had Known

I had an aunt named Pat. She suffered a very messy divorce and vowed she would never marry again. Being the superstitious person that she was, she went to see a clairvoyant who told her that on the upcoming Saturday she would meet a man named David, fall in love and marry him. Shortly after, a friend of hers announced that she was having a party and she wanted my aunty Pat to meet a friend of hers, named David. And so, she didn't go.

People are always saying 'if only they had known' as if life would be better if we knew the consequences of everything we did. I disagree. I say to all those people who say, 'if only they had known', 'If only you had known you didn't need to know'. Now, by now I am sure many people here are thinking 'if only I had known what she was talking about'. And quite understandably. Well, I would be right in saying you are now paying more attention to what I am saying and that is the point I am trying to make. Because you don't know what on earth I am talking about, you are inspired to try and find out. Not knowing drives us on. Not knowing inspires curiosity and curiosity leads us to making discoveries, and discoveries generally make our lives better or at least more interesting. I believe that it is curiosity and not knowing that drives us on. After all, what is the point of reading the book if you already know what happens in the end? As soon as we know, we lose interest and there is nothing to keep us focused. I mean think of all the wonderful things we have discovered because we didn't know about something.

What is it that baffles us all? It is love. That cutesy frame of mind we all fall in and out of periodically. In the *Sydney Morning Herald* last year, it was reported that a group of Italian scientists have discovered that falling in love could actually be a mental illness. The group found, after testing a selection of self-confessed cupid victims, that there was a similar chemical imbalance in their brains as is found in those suffering with Obsessive, compulsive disorder. Dr Marazziti told *New Scientist* magazine 'It's often said that when you're in love, you're a little bit crazy. That may be true.' You see it is the things that we know nothing about—I mean who can honestly say they understand love—it is these things that we know absolutely nothing about that are teaching us valuable lessons about ourselves. The unknown inspires us and drives us towards valuable discoveries.

Millions of dollars are spent every year on the study of the great out there as astronomers desperately search for intelligent life. One thing that we know next to nothing about and therefore are completely obsessed with is space. It is a part of science that it publicised, televised, created into movies and sponsored. Yes, the incredible hype that surrounds the biggest unknown of all—space was recognised by Pizza Hut last year. In mid-November last year, one of Russia's Proton rockets blasted off into space with a 10-m-high Pizza Hut logo displayed on the front of the rocket. You see Pizza Hut have realised the power of the curiosity surrounding the big unknown. Their plan is to continue their space age marketing plan by sending up pizzas in subsequent voyages. Now if this all sounds a little unnecessary, well we should be grateful it only went so far as the 10-m logo. The initial idea that Pizza Hut were hoping to achieve was to have its logo projected by lasers onto the moon. But that's not all. They also wanted the jingle: 'When the moon hits your eye like a big pizza pie. Pizza Hut.' Tacky, I know. But can you blame them. Space is one of the largest grossing, publicised and respected industries in the world. The great unknown certainly gets our attention.

But let's look at the other side of the coin. What happens when people do know.

An example of knowing destroying everything is *The Nanny*. Yes, I am talking about the American soap starring and directed by Fran Drescher. Do you remember just how popular this show was? It had fantastic ratings. It was one of those wonderful shows that everyone watched but never admitted to watching. It was popular until Fran married Mr Sheffield. Then, we all knew too much. There was nothing left to find out and so there was no reason to watch and so no one did. The ratings more than halved after the wedding episode. If only they had known we didn't want to know.

Despite the obvious advancements that the unknown has effectively given us and putting aside the fact that the biggest problem people have with the unknown is that they don't understand it, people may still say that there are some things that you just have to know. And that there are some things that simply would have worked out better if people had known. This may be true for some of the time, but unfortunately it is not true for a great deal of the time. In February last year a toddler died from neglect. He died despite the fact that DOCS, the organisation in charge of these things, had been notified of his situation three times. When this case was looked into in June last year, it was not DOCS that ended up looking bad, but instead the government. DOCS revealed that they were so underfunded that they had to prioritise cases. In fact, they can only afford to take action on 5% of the cases that they are notified about. That means that unless a child is being sexually or physically abused, then they have no hope of being helped. So, it doesn't matter who knows or who can claim to have known, nothing more can be done. Another dimension was added to this sad case when the government themselves confessed 'If only we had known'. They did know, or they could have found out, it just wasn't on the top of their list of priorities. They were too fixated by whatever was on the top of their list they didn't think to look. In some ways, saying 'If only they had known' is just an excuse. In my opinion it is an excuse that should never have to be made, especially when it comes to people, especially young children. We should be living each day, doing what is right and what is needed not just because we know about something or just because it is on the top of the list of priorities, but because it is something that needs to be done. So, knowing does not always mean that the right thing will be done.

And knowing too much, or at least thinking you know too much can do more harm than good. You may remember at the start of last year a 14-year-old found herself in a rather unfortunate position. She became agoraphobic. This means that you find open or unfamiliar spaces terrifying; as a result, most people cannot leave their homes. The reason for this was that she rang up a clairvoyant hotline and was told that she would be killed sometime in the next 6 months. The result of the incident was outrage on behalf of the government and people alike. New rules, enforcement and age limits were laid down as people tried to control how much people could claim to know.

If only they had known. It seems life is better if you just live it. If you let the big out there and curiosity drive you on, then you will find out more than you could ever imagine. Things like love are completely unknown to us and that is the fun of living. Not knowing what it is you are doing. After all it seems that even if something is known about—it doesn't mean it gets done. And knowing the future can spoil the present. It seems to me that we should live each day as it comes. *Que sara sara*—what ever will be, will be.

Do you remember my aunty Pat, the one who turned down going to the party in case of falling in love? Well, she too knew the merits of the unknown. When she passed away, her ashes were put in a firework, and she was let off into space.

So, what I would like to say to all those people who live their lives saying 'If only they had known' is if only *you* had known, you didn't *need* to know.

Knowing When to Quit

Since the age of five I have seen some horrible addictions. Kindergarten saw the rise of the infamous skipping rope, I saw many young girls jump away all their lunch time, but due to a lack of co-ordination I resisted. Next, in year three came yo-yos, many of my friends tried some pretty hard stuff at this time—cat's cradle, walking the dog ... but I never succumb to peer pressure. After that many more Mattel products hit the schoolyard; I saw many children suffer as they didn't know when to quit—but I never once gave in. But now in year 11 there is a new trend. One I can't resist. I want a mobile phone. I want to understand what people are saying when they tell me they have a Nokia 5110. I want to be like the rest of Australia and key the *Mission Impossible* theme in as my ring. And most importantly I want to just

once be the embarrassed party who is forced to exit the movies because they forgot to turn their mobile off. It's sad, it's pathetic—I am not proud. But how did I stand a chance. We have taken gimmicky technology too far and if we don't quit now then there will be even more people in the desperate state I find myself in.

Ladies and Gentlemen, a significant proportion of technology is becoming useless, tacky and incredibly addictive. It is needless to say that there are some fantastic examples of technology doing great things for us but there is also a lot doing quite the opposite. People are constantly saying people should quit smoking because it is bad for your health —I agree, but I also think the same applies when it comes to tacky technological things that go beep. It seems that these things are seriously endangering our health in Australia.

Mobile phones are taking over, science is dictated by commercialisation and the internet is becoming a moralistic hole. But I am talking about knowing when to quit. Well, I also know that the time to quit tacky technology is now. In fact, it seems to me that all those warnings that they place on cigarette packages also apply to a lot of today's technologies.

Take the mobile phone for example. Although a mobile is necessary some of the time and for some people, it is not for half the people that have them. They are tacky and they may be associated with brain cancer. **Today's technology can cause cancer.** Two million and 877 thousand Australian households have at least one mobile phone. One million 988 thousand and 100 have at least one child. Yes, there are more mobiles per household than children. All these people *need* their mobile phone? No, of course not, it is the accessory of the 21st century, to be cool, hip and trendy you have to have one. Most people will have seen the cartoon of two men comparing mobile phones the caption being 'Mine's smaller than yours'. Why is the mobile so popular with our generation? Well, it is reasonably cheap, it's new, it's plastic, it comes in different colours, it goes beep—is it any wonder they are hard to quit? Mobile phones are convenient, and this convenience of being able to call anyone at any time equals power, power that can be dangerous in the 21st century. You see today achieving that 15 seconds of fame is seen as very important—something to get before you die and so the power of a mobile phone can prove too much for some. On 21 April last year, as you are all no doubt aware, there was a shooting at the Columbine high school. Hiding away in the bushes for safety a young boy with a mobile phone waits. Who does he call? The Police? No. An ambulance? No. His parents? Heaven forbid! No! He rings a television station. This tacky technology is starting to take over our lives. Governing what we do and how we do it. It is time we quit this superficial technology.

Today's technology can be addictive. It seems to me that half of what we are using today's great advancements for is futile, and we are just doing it for the sake of using technology. I mean it seems to be that the operations which occupy scientific technology is almost completely commercialised. I mean Coke, the fizzy drink, has done what the

United Nations could never do and provided something that unites almost every country in the world. Well, it has just gone interstellar. Yes, COKE have a drink dispenser in space. I doubt it has made a lot of money since it went up there in 1995, but hey, it gives Americans pride to think that they have literally taken their fast food to new heights. Science and space technology have been beneficial and could be even more beneficial if we put it to better and more scientific use. For our own sake we need to let go of these superficial things, because it is time we quit, and give up this superficial technology.

So, what is another great example of today's fantastic technology? It is, of course, the internet. Well, it seems through the internet Today's **Technology can harm your baby.** Ron's chicks operate over the internet. Now the point of Ron's chicks is to sell eggs, not the conventional farmyard model. No, Ron specializes in people eggs for artificial insemination. Ron offers his customers the opportunity to choose from a list of donors that are 'beautiful people'. By beautiful people I mean models who have spent half their life throwing up their breakfasts. The biggest problem here, in my opinion, is if this idea catches on, aren't we going to have a slightly limited range of people? I mean if everyone starts to mail order a child of a model sure we will be beautiful, but will we ever get anything done? After all, where would our society be if it weren't for all those incredibly smart people. I mean, is Bill Gates complaining? If we are not careful, the useless bits of today's technology are going to interfere with our children and subsequently our future. It is time to quit.

But this is not the only problem. **Today's technology should not be sold to persons under the age of 18.** I am sure most people here are aware of all the moralistic dilemmas and questions surrounding the Internet. There is so much that is so accessible and so much that really shouldn't be so accessible. I had my own taste of this when I was 13 and trying to research a project on 'the Greek Gods'. Boy did I find some 'Greek Gods'—just not the ones I was looking for. It seems to me that there is no real successful censoring system and no real intention of finding one, we are so preoccupied with progression and where the Internet can go, that we are no longer interested in addressing these ethical issues and protecting our children. The time to quit this tacky technology is now.

So Ladies and Gentlemen; try to cut down to one phone call a day, don't get hooked on a drink unless it is on this planet and never let minors visit www.GreekGods.com. Because maybe if we all start to go cold turkey on superficial technology then perhaps we can quit for good.

So, the question I now ask myself is do I really want a mobile phone?

Because if I don't start, I won't have to worry about knowing when to quit.

Good Fences Make Good Neighbours

A year four teacher was asked to present, with her class, a dramatised version of a fairy tale for a teaching conference. After much discussion, they decided on Cinderella because it had a large number of defined characters that guaranteed every child a part. The parts were allocated to everyone except one boy. The teacher asked him 'Norman, who do you want to be?' Norman replied, 'I would like to be the pig'. The teacher was quite confused; there was no pig in Cinderella. She tried to explain to Norman that 'There is no pig in Cinderella' but he just said, 'There is now'.

Today people like to define everyone. We like to fit all people into nicely defined, expectable roles that everyone is familiar with. I mean there is a Prince in Cinderella—that we can all cope with, but a pig? We like to build fences around people and the space they occupy so that they are well defined. But the problem is, good fences don't make good neighbours, people do. We are so busy trying to define people, but do we actually appreciate them? It seems as though we are losing touch with the true value of a human being. We are getting [so] preoccupied with money, the face value of things and historical records, that we forget what is really important. We need to step back and appreciate people for what they are truly worth. We need to stop trying to fence people in and instead appreciate them.

Often, we build fences for financial reasons. In our money-obsessed, statistic rating world the biggest question of all is—what is the price of life? Well, believe it or not, the Bureau of Transport Economics has found the answer. You are worth $859,030. After the incredible number of road crashes last year, the bureau decided to work out, using a theoretical or a statistical life, what the price of a human being is. An average life they decided, was worth $319,030 for quality plus $540,000 in lost labour. I don't know about you, but I find this a little insulting. Is that all a human being is? $319,030 worth of quality? And what does it say about our society that the price put on lost labour is nearly double this amount? I also think that here in Australia we must be getting a pretty bad deal because when the same study was done in America, they decided people were worth $5.5 million. The Director of the Bureau of Transport Economics said: 'People generally value their own lives very highly, indeed, life can be argued to be priceless, as without life money would be of no use'. This is ridiculous! You can't put a price on a human being. The bureau claimed they did the study because of the number of road deaths last year—surely this should be our focus and we should be working out how to save people not how to put a price tag on them. How to help people, not how to fence them in.

But we often get carried away with the face-value of things. We focus on what the fence is made out of and how it looks, rather than the neighbour inside. We get so carried away with how we define something—the exact wording, that we forget about the meaning. The English language is a very confusing thing. To make it even worse, we have had the onset of the feminist approach of 'we have burnt the bra now let's turn on the dictionary'. All words are being forced into non-gender specific forms. Now this would be fine, I mean some people do feel offended by how they are described, but it is getting out of hand. And to be perfectly honest, I don't really see the point in a lot of cases, as it is generally not the words used that give away whether a person is male or female. Today people are paranoid about their choice of words, to the degree where it is socially compulsory to blush as you say 'human'. But the truth of the matter is, 'Man' is not actually gender specific at all. It comes from the old English 'mann' spelt with a double n, and it means people. People in general. So, in other words, all those raving feminists who refuse to be part of humanity—are simply saying that they are not people at all. You see it's not the words or how we define people that is important, its not the fence that is important, but rather the neighbour inside. What is important is that we are all human. We are all people and as valuable as each other—no matter what we may be called.

What I personally believe is the worst case of fence building of all, is when people feel it is so necessary to tell the world about some cause or incident that they don't actually help. When people think that building a fence is so important that they don't realise that their neighbour needs them. I mean how many times have you seen a photo of a starving child? It has to be one of the most looked at, talked about and publicised images in the world today. We are so familiar with photos of children in pain or suffering. I came across a photo of a young girl drowning—and it struck me, couldn't the photographer have done something? Most people in the Western world can swim or at least throw in a rope—could this photographer not? Many claim that photographers are only there to observe—only to build a fence, not to interfere. But where does the role of the photographer end? As a photographer maybe they shouldn't interfere—but as human beings, how could they not? Most people are familiar with Nick Ut's photo of a young girl running on fire. It struck me, he made a lot of money, the 9-year-old girl burned. But then I found out a little more about the photo, Nick Ut, the man who took the photo, showed how it was possible to observe and help. A while after he had taken the photo and it had become successful, he returned to Vietnam and found the girl, and helped her medically and to get an education. What he realised is that although he may have presented something historically valuable to the world—what was important was the person, not the fence. We need to stop trying to define people, trying to show the world who people are or what is happening to them and trying to build fences around them, and instead value them for what they are worth. And help if necessary.

Good fences don't make good neighbours, people do. How we define people isn't important. We need to stop trying to fence people in and instead appreciate them because they are priceless. We are priceless, despite what the Bureau of Transport Economics may tell us. It's also not the way we define people that is important, but rather that we appreciate everybody. Finally, while historical records and news reports are valuable, I feel that helping people, supporting people and appreciating people is more important. We need to stop trying to define people, trying to build fences around them, and instead value them for what they are worth. Good fences don't make good neighbours, people do.

Do you remember that production of Cinderella with Norman the pig? Well, the teacher let Norman play the pig, but he had to work out his own part. So, he followed Cinderella

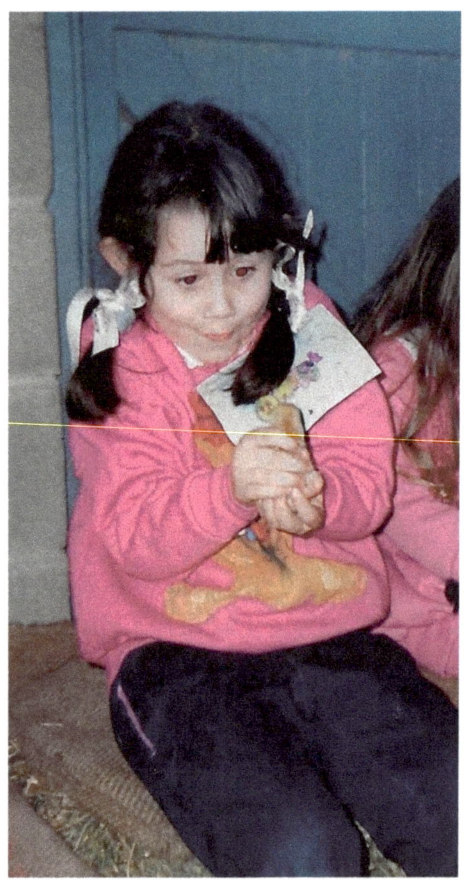

around for the duration of the play. His facial expressions reflected the action. When it was sad, he frowned, when it was happy, he smiled and when it was a little confusing—Norman looked confused. At the very end, as Cinderella and her prince ran off to their happy ending, Norman the pig danced around the stage and barked. The teacher had tried to explain that pigs didn't bark, but Norman just said, 'This one did'. The play was performed and the Norman the barking pig got a standing ovation. Every time the class performed the teacher explained that this was an unusual production of Cinderella because it had a barking pig in it. People would say 'but there is no pig in Cinderella', so she would reply 'There is now'. People make life fun and interesting, it doesn't matter if you can't put a defined fence around them. After all good fences don't make good neighbours, people do.

To Win

In the *New York Times magazine*, July 1992, appeared a photo. A photo of a middle-aged man by the name of Vedran Smailovic. He was dressed in formal evening clothes; he was sitting in the middle of a street, in front of a bakery where a mortar fire killed 22 people waiting in a line for bread in late May. Not only is he sitting in this precarious position, but he is playing the cello. He is a member of the Sarajevo Opera Orchestra. He is a musician and there is very little he can do about hate and war—it has been going on in Sarajevo for centuries. Although there is so much chaos and hate around him, he still takes a chance and every day sits near that bakery and plays an Adagio in G minor. He can achieve no personal gain from risking his life and sitting in the middle of a war. He cannot win. He does not need the will to win. He has something more important, the will to keep going. *The will to win is not as important as most people think. What is more important is the will to keep on going. To keep on going even if there is apparently nothing you can gain. You see ladies and gentlemen if you have the will to keep on going you never know, you might just win.*

When you look at my smile, what do you see? You see braces. Two strips of metal fastened between my lips. I got my braces on last March and let me tell you these past 15 months have been absolute ... hell. Within three days of getting my braces on I wanted them off. OK, we are talking pain here. When I first got them on, I could not even put my teeth within a centimetre from each other without screaming. I lost 5 kilos in the first three days I had my braces on and it really didn't help when I showed my grandfather: 'Look Grandad, I've got braces!' And he said, 'Never mind, we still love you'. But I'll let you in on a little secret. They're coming off. Yes, last Tuesday I went to see my orthodontist and he told me that I could have them off soon. I can't wait. I have spent the last 15 months with a few bits of cutlery stuck in my mouth and let me tell you that took quite a bit of will power. When you are sitting in that dentist's chair with someone sticking pliers in your mouth knowing that by doing this you are beating no one, you are not going to find great wealth—in fact quite the opposite as braces are not cheap, all that is important is the will to keep on going. By having the will to keep on going you gain something that I believe is even better than winning—satisfaction. Before I got my braces on I thought that I was not going to win anything by having them but now I appreciate that in a sense I have won. I have won satisfaction.

In India there is great poverty, there is great hate and a lot of pain. People are suffering in a situation that appears to have no good, no comfort and no hope of ever resolving. However, there is one who had the will to keep on going. One slightly wrinkled, rather short woman dressed in a blue sari—Mother Theresa who brought hope to India and that there was some comfort and some good. She showed this by selflessly helping people. She had no race to try and win. There was nothing that she could gain from risking disease and facing death everyday and yet she did. She kept going. She has now passed on. She will never have gained great wealth or any of the other things that most people associate with winning, but I guess in a way, as a result of her will to keep on helping, she did win. She had the satisfaction of helping others in a selfless way and leaving the world truly inspired.

My mother used to teach a class of children with learning difficulties. She had one student called Ben who had a severe learning difficulty. He had trouble focusing on one thing so the small task of holding a crayon and drawing seemed impossible. My mother had the will to teach but he had the will to keep on going until he became quite an artist. In this class there was also a girl called Alice who has a heart defect and could not walk very far without falling over. Every time she fell, she would get the standard response 'oopsy daisy, up you get'. She had the will to keep on going. Every time she fell. From this constant repetition she would say 'oopsy daisy, up you get'. *Oopsy daisy up you get*. This just about summarises the will to keep on going. Even when all seems hopeless and you are lying on the floor or in a dentist chair, as the case may be, to say *oopsy daisy* and to get back up required a very strong will. The will to keep on going.

1998

The Ultimate Insanity

Since the beginning of time humanity has had an obsession with size in all realms of life. Ancient man must have gone to incredible lengths to create great big things like the Pyramids, Stonehenge and the Great Wall of China. The question you have to ask yourself is why? What is the point of suffering, pain and hardship for something big when something a lot smaller would do the job just as well? Preoccupation with size is the ultimate insanity. Today however we are not only obsessed with big things but also really small things.

As the human race we have built many large things. They all seemed like a good idea at the time, and for some strange reason some of them have even made some money and turned into tourism attractions. We have created the giant pineapple, the big prawn and my personal favourite, the big banana. However, not all 'big things' are quite so productive. In Britain they spent $20 million on a giant pink lady. Surprisingly enough, no one in Britain wanted to walk through this oversized woman. No doubt you are thinking 'well that's what you get for being stupid enough to build a big woman and then paint it pink'. Well, the truth is, the pink lady was in fact built by a group of Australians—the same group responsible for the other big pink thing, the Big Prawn. To make matters worse, because this big thing has turned into a black hole in the tourism industry in Britain, they want to send it back to Australia. The idea is that it will become part of that other great insanity that is the Olympic. The question you have to ask yourself is why. Why do we think size is so wonderful that people are going to pay to see 'big things'? More importantly why do people pay to see 'big things'? It is the ultimate insanity.

But it is not just big things we are obsessed with. As anorexia and bulimia have become fashionable pastimes; it seems that miniscule is just as good as incredibly big. We have laptop computers, microchips and mobile phones so small that if you happen to have hair longer than your ears it looks as though you are talking to yourself. I mean most people will have seen the cartoon of two men comparing their mobile phones, the caption being 'mine's smaller than yours'. Why do we do it? Is it because we as a population feel inadequate? Do we think that we are failing as a species and therefore feel the need to stare at oversized fruit while talking on tiny phones?

Big fish eat little fish. In fact, big fish eat whole schools of little fish. We seem to be drawing ever closer to the unfortunate situation where we no longer have countries, instead we have companies. I mean at the rate we are going, it would seem it won't be long before the southern and northern hemispheres are distinguishable by the fact that one is owned by Coke and the other McDonald's. Or maybe Nike and Reebok. Or perhaps simply Packer and Murdoch. But Microsoft and Apple have a pretty strong grip on the world. Although it really wouldn't surprise me if they were all owned by Burger King and the earth turned into one giant fast-food franchise. Big is taking over. Greengrocers are a dying breed as Franklins dominates and swallows up competition, but is this really a good step? We are losing the personal touch despite how often Woolworths assure us that they are the 'fresh food people'. In fact, Mitsubishi earns 140 billion US dollars. That is more than Poland, more than Greece, South Africa, Malaysia, Israel, Columbia, Venezuela and the Philippines. This is not healthy. The biggest problem with these large companies is that they have the money and resources to exploit countries that have very little trade and union regulations and then they take their product to countries that have very strong unions and make a hell of a lot of money. It is not right. It is commercial domination. The new religion is commercial imperialism. In fact, studies have shown that the McDonald's golden arches are more recognisable than the crucifix. Big is not better.

In fact, sacrificing ourselves to big things has to go down as one of the greatest insanities.

It is insane, in fact preoccupation with size is the ultimate insanity because as we all know, it's not size that is important, but what you do with it.

Tall Poppies or Tall Weeds

There was a young girl. I have chosen to omit the names to protect the innocent. This little girl, like most young girls, desperately wanted to be a ballerina. She joined a ballet class and every Friday afternoon for two hours she twirled and pliéd, leapt and pointed. The little girl soon turned out to be quite ... hopeless. The end of year dance approached. It was of a flower motif. The little girl desperately wanted to be a tall poppy, and wear a pretty red tutu, but when the dance was cast, the little girl was a weed. Not only was she a weed, but she was the one and only weed.

Many people believe that it is the people who are glorified, the people who get to wear the pretty red tutus, the tall poppies of the world, which are truly successful. I beg to differ. It seems to me that the truly successful people are the people who go about, doing what they can and what they think is right. It is the tall weeds that are the backbone of our society. You see while the tall poppies have glory, the tall weeds actually do something. Tall weeds are people like lollipop persons. They are the people that let you cut in front of them in Franklins because they have a whole trolley, and you have one item. They are the foreign aid workers who we know of, but don't know their names. You see tall weeds actually help people, you don't know their names or even what it is they are doing—but they are still helping people and most importantly it seems to be the tall weeds who selflessly reach out to those who need help.

It is tall weeds that actually get things done, and actually help people. Take Ernest Ridding for example. Now most people here are probably thinking who on earth is he, and that is my point. Ernest Ridding is a tall weed. Most probably close to nobody here has ever heard of him. He has in fact written an autobiography *Self Portrait of a Nut.* Mr Ridding is doing great things for those living in poverty in Sydney. He is 'the Glebe fridge man'. He has repaired around 3000 fridges from his Housing Department home and given them to the needy. He is now broadening his horizons and repairing computers as well. He is not government funded, he does not have an ad campaign. When he gives away one of his fridges the 7:30 Report isn't there to film it—he is not glorified, instead he is just doing what he thinks is right and as a result he is helping people and doing good things for our city. He is a *tall weed,* and he is proud.

But everyday there are people doing good yet unglorified things. There are people who sort our clothes for charities and people who help little old ladies across the street. I have an elderly friend who recently suffered a stroke. Her greatest regret is not that she can no longer go about doing her own shopping and so forth, but that she has had to give up the thing which meant most to her. Every Wednesday she would catch a taxi to a hostel and read to children with severe disabilities. Half of them hardly seemed to notice she was there, but when she didn't come, they used to suffer from anxiety and general distress.

Very often, the *tall weed* so to speak is the last person you would expect. I was surprised, when at my great uncle's funeral, I found out that he used to drive children with Downs Syndrome to group activities. My surprise soon led to a sense of great respect, as it was something good that he just did without praise from other people, without pay or encouragement—it was just something he enjoyed. When you enter a garden, it is not the tall weeds that you notice, or that take your breath away with their exquisite beauty—but they are still there and growing strong.

Overall, in the world every day horrible things are happening, and people are in pain. While we hear of some of the glorified help that is aimed at fixing these problems, we do not hear of some of the most beneficial things going on. I do not by any means wish to debase the help some of these organisations are bringing, but it seems to me that there is a significant amount of good being done by people and organisations that do not get the glory. Take Catherine Hamlin for example. She and her late husband were both gynecologists. Dr Hamlin worked in the depths of Ethiopia. In the poverty-stricken Ethiopian society, if a young girl suffers an internal injury whilst giving birth—most of the girls are around 16—they are left by their husbands, by their families and their communities ... for dead. It is not because their communities are uncaring—they will have the deepest sympathies for the young girl—they just don't understand. Most young girls give birth from their own homes; when something does go wrong, all that anyone there can recognize is that she can produce no more children and, in most cases, appears crippled. So, she is left for dead. In other words, girls my age are left to die, to die of something that can be fixed with a very simple operation, The two Dr Hamlins recognized how terrible and unnecessary this situation was, and so found funding for themselves and set up a small hospital in 1974. Since then, over 18,000 girls have not only been helped but also given a new boost and chance at life. But now this *tall weed* operation is receiving support from *Tall Poppy*

SYDNEY WEEKLY Issue 29

16th October, 2003   **Web:** www.plc.nsw.edu.au

From the Principal...

Dear Parents,

The school community is saddened at the passing of Kathryn Carter due to a sudden illness, on Saturday 4th October, 2003. Her funeral, attended by over five hundred people was held at Drummoyne Presbyterian Church, where she taught Sunday school.

Kathryn completed her Higher School Certificate in 2001, after seven years as a student at PLC. Kathryn was a School Prefect. Her time at PLC was spent in many endeavours, ranging from sport to art and to that which she is best remembered - the stage and the podium.

Kathryn Carter - PLC '01

Kathryn devoted many hours to representing both school and state in public speaking competitions and eisteddfods, the likes of which included IGSSC; Plain English Speaking; Senior Oratories and her favourite, Rostrum. She also achieved Grade 8 level in Speech and Drama Examinations at Trinity College, London and ASCA. The pinnacle of her speaking career came with the award of the inaugural ASCA Scholarship in 2001. Kathryn was a master of impromptu speaking and a keen debater, often giving her time to coach and encourage younger students.

For those that saw Kathryn perform on stage, she will be remembered for 'Adelaide' in *Guys and Dolls*; *Annie* and *Godspell*, and major roles in Shakespeare's *Othello, Julius Caesar, King Lear, Romeo & Juliet, Midsummer Night's Dream* as well as 'Antigone' and her very memorable HSC Drama Work adapted from Dorothy Porter.

Kathryn never really left PLC. She remained a debating coach and active member of the ex-students union, of which her mother, Helen Carter, is President. This was in addition to her studies as an Arts student at The University of Sydney and the recent formation of her own drama school, Cheshire Drama.

While Kathryn will be remembered as an accomplished young woman, those that were lucky enough to know her will cherish her smile, her vibrancy, her loyalty and the sheer joy she took in living life to the fullest.

We offer our deepest sympathy and prayers to Helen and John Carter, Kathryn's parents.

Kathryn will be greatly missed. She has left us for a time, yet will remain in our hearts forever.

organisations, as the Australian government and some charity organisations including World Vision sponsor them. It is fantastic to see the tall poppies join together with the tall weeds. Because while I have been showing you all the true worth of tall weeds—there really is nothing wrong with a bit of glory—after all, it is often very closely attached to money. Perhaps if we let one big garden grow, complete with poppies <u>and</u> weeds—both just as tall as the other then perhaps we would have glory and get things done.

But never forget the true worth of *tall weeds*, after all, they have the power to overshadow a whole bed of poppies. It is *tall weeds* that do simple things like repairing fridges—just to help people. Very often no one even knows the good that these *tall weeds* are doing—but they do it anyway. And most importantly it is the *tall weeds* that selflessly help others. Although, all can be assisted by a little glory. But it is the *tall weeds* that get things done in our society.

Do you remember that little girl who played the part of the Weed in the ballet? Well, the night of the big dance came. It was an utter disaster. One dancer tripped and all the apparently talented poppies fell in a sort of domino formation. The only one left standing was the weed. Silence. Then one man up the back stood up and cheered 'Let's hear it for the Weed!' So, the little girl did a simple turn and the whole place erupted with cheering and general applause. The dance was a slight success, thanks to the weed.

You see it is far better to be standing upright at the end of the day, than to be wearing a red tutu, because no matter how pretty it is, it won't look good if you end up with your legs in the air.

Tackiness Is Taking Over

In Column 8 of the *Sydney Morning Herald* in April a conversation in a Sydney café was described. One woman questioned the other on a recent relationship, the reply was 'Well, he has entered me into his mobile phone so I guess we are an item'.

Ladies and gentlemen, Tackiness is taking over. Those artificial, superficial things that we do not really need but can't seem to live without are starting to govern our lives, judgments and opinions. We are losing sight of what is real, what is important and more importantly, who we are. When it comes down to it we are becoming very superficial. So what is Tacky? On this subject opinion does vary; my mother thinks blue mascara is great, I disagree. Tacky is artificial and is not necessary for everyday life but is still commonly used.

A mobile phone is a good example. Although a mobile is necessary some of the time and for some people, it is not for half the people that have them. Two million and 877 thousand Australian households have at least one mobile phone. One million 988 thousand and 100 have at least one child. Yes there are more mobiles per household than children. All these people *need* their mobile phone? No, it is the accessory of the 90s, to be cool, hip and trendy you need one. Most people will have seen the cartoon of two men comparing mobile phones the caption being 'Mine's smaller than yours'.

Why is the mobile so popular to people in the 90s? Well, it is reasonably cheap, it's new, it is plastic, it comes in different colours, it goes beep—what more could you ask? The attraction to the 'mobile' is not unlike the attraction people felt towards those novelty phones that were oh so popular in the 80s. You remember the time when you couldn't tell whether it was the shoe or the cat that was ringing. At this point in time you could get a phone in any shape, size or cartoon character you liked. I ask you ladies and gentlemen, how are you supposed to have a deep and meaningful or even slightly serious conversation when you are talking to Snoopy's rear end.

Mobile phones are convenient, and this convenience of being able to call anyone at anytime equals power, power that can be dangerous in the 90s. You see today achieving that 15 seconds of fame is seen as very important—something to get before you die and so the power of a mobile phone can prove too much for some. On the 21st of April this year, as you are all no doubt aware, there was a shooting at a Columbine high school in America. Hiding away in the bushes for safety a young boy with a mobile phone waits. Who does he call? The police? An ambulance? His parents? Heaven forbid! No, he rings a television station. These tacky things are starting to take over our lives. Governing what we do and how we do it.

Saturday April the tenth was the day to get lucky if you wanted a baby for the turn of the millennium or if you wanted a million dollars for that matter. On this date all over the world competitions promising up to and over a million dollars were being offered to the couple that has the pleasure of writing themselves into the history books by having the first baby of the millennium. Family planning experts are not nearly as concerned about the Millennium bug at the moment as they are in far too much of a panic about this Millennium baby. In Britain, the family planning association has gone so far that they have plastered 'A baby is for life, not just for the millennium' on billboards across the country. The thought that the fact human life must be considered as more than just a gimmick has to be pointed out to people in writing several metres tall is terrifying. Tackiness is taking over. That superficial, fame-seeking part that lurks in all of us is starting to dominate. Staring to govern our common sense—changing our opinions, guiding our morals and dominating our judgements.

Many claim we are living in the time of technological advances—science is apparently at its peak. It seems to me that tackiness has corrupted this branch of life as well. Millions of dollars is spent every year on the observation of the big out there as astronomers search for intelligent life. So what is the product of this massive operation? Well, they have discovered a smiley face on Mars. Yes, in the week of Saturday March the 13th this year the NASA spacecraft that is floating around above our heads at this very moment happily snapping away, mapping the red planet sent back photos of this 'Happy face crater'. I mean come on. It is a completely foreign place to us, surely we should be looking at and discussing something that cannot be found on tee shirts all over the world. Even the judgement of people who have degrees are being corrupted by tackiness.

Not only this but it seems that our government is being equally superficial, immature and acting like an oversize teenager who is obsessed with the tacky. After all no tacky obsessed high school student can hold their head up in public without petty and basically silly ideas about who is entitled to sit where at oh, I don't know, a popular sporting event. No teenager can rightfully claim the position and title of frustrated youth without arguments that focus more on the idea of who is going to apologise first as opposed to what the actual problem is. And of course no young adult can strut their stuff unless they are in the middle of making a decision of where they stand in regards to their family, where they belong and how independent they are.

Some may argue that it is our rite of passage and we are in fact becoming more independent and are becoming more serious, sensible and mature by our discussions and indeed the vote regarding the republican issue. Others argue that the only reason we even touched on the subject in the manner we did and only addressed the issue in the first place was for the sake of how other countries see us. In other words we were simply being preoccupied with the superficial—what others thought of us.

To me the epitome of tackiness is our Olympic mascots. I mean we have Syd—a rather terrifying kookaburra, Ollie a rather odd-looking Koala and Millie the buxom Platypus. These three deformed Blinky Bill rejects are going to represent not only Sydney but

Australia to the world? I mean look at the first attempt we had, Kangaroos on bicycles. I mean please. An Australian in America was asked which state of the USA Australia was in. The Olympics is our chance to show them we are a country and we do not walk on our heads and we choose three very, very, very ugly cartoon characters to do this? Where is our self-esteem? Where is our pride? Where is our self-respect for crying out loud? It is there somewhere, somewhere under the masses of McDonald's induced tackiness. Yes I blame America. All those years of being force-fed *The Simpsons*, *Saved by the Bell*, *Oprah*, *Ricky Lake* and *Baywatch* are leading us towards becoming a perfect replica of that great tacky land that is America. The land where large Cokes are big enough to feed a small family.

Yes the real thing. The fizzy drink that has done what the United Nations could never do and provided something that unites almost every country in the world. The advancements made by NASA and the discoveries made by scientists all over the world are fantastic. They have mapped planets, calculated immense distances and found many ingenious ways of looking for intelligent life. Well that is nothing. COKE have a drink dispenser in space. What can't Americans do? Where can't they take their fast food? Because I feel we are steadily losing our identity not only to America but also American-influenced small plastic creatures and products, I really respect the people in Avalon. Those poor people were put down, harassed, emotionally blackmailed and basically bagged out simply because they did not want David Hasselhoff running around with Pamela Lee Anderson in their backyard for six months of the year. Can you imagine that? Once you had got over the initial glamour and other appeals that those red swimmers may hold—or not as the case maybe—having the *Baywatch* crew at your doorstep would simply be irritating. You couldn't leave your house for fear of being caught at one of your more delicate moments on international television. So good luck to Hawaii—enjoy those red floaty things.

In conclusion ladies and gentlemen, do not let tackiness guide your life. Please do not be one of those people who let their mobile ring at the most crucial point of a movie or for that matter, never test out all the different rings you can program into your mobile in a café. Remember your morals and basic ideals, even when someone waves a million dollars in your face. Do not rely on a billboard to tell you what to do. Put our resources to a good use and never do anything just because of how it looks to other people. And above all never lose your identity to a character that even Blinky Bill rejected. Do not let tackiness guide your life, judgments and opinions. Hold on to the things that make us Australians and basically humans for that matter—if we don't, heaven forbid, tackiness may take over completely and leave us looking like Americans living in an eternal sitcom.

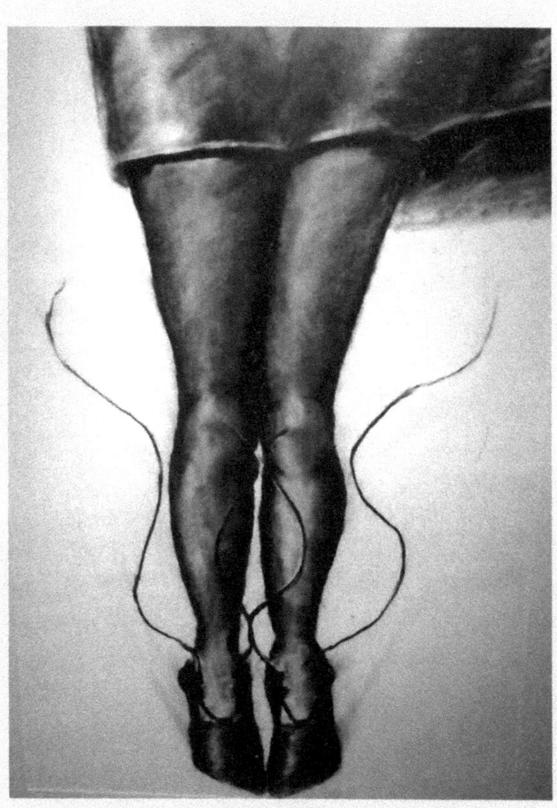

We Are Only Visiting

Some family friends of ours have a little boy called Joshua who can't handle the word 'good-bye'. My mother discovered this a couple of weekends ago when Joshua visited our house and then burst into tears as my mother wished him good-bye. Our friends explained that a short time ago, Joshua had had a friend come to play, he had such a good time with this friend that he didn't want him to leave. But, when his mother made him wish his friend good-bye, he did leave, and they hadn't got round to seeing him since. Basically, what Joshua can't yet grasp is the concept of 'we are only visiting'. This isn't really a problem, and you really can't hold it against him as he hasn't even reached the grand age of two yet. But still, to be perfectly honest, I don't blame him. I am in year twelve and certainly can't handle the thought that soon I am going to leave the school world and enter into the big scary land of grown-ups.

It seems that we are only ever visiting, because nothing is forever. This all seems a little obvious, I know, and it is something we all take for granted, but it wasn't until I started thinking about this concept that it dawned on me, just how temporary everything is. From the natural fact that people are born, and people die to all the scientific advances being made, to the fact that due to continental drifting, the very country we are standing on is eroding away. This is huge. It is mind-boggling. It may sound obvious to say 'things are always progressing' but have you ever thought just how mammoth this fact is? We only ever seem to be visiting anywhere, we are constantly advancing in every possible way. We have made so many fantastic advancements because people have been determined to assist in something about the world. Because they have helped us progress. Aside from this, in the majority of cases change is simply inevitable, and out of our control. Unfortunately, there is one element to this concept of 'nothing is forever' that is never a particularly happy occasion, and that is the death of a loved one. I believe that we should embrace the fact that we are only visiting and take hold of every opportunity. After all, places you only visit are far more enjoyable. 'We are only visiting' so we should not only enjoy what we have, while we have it, but also look forward to the next place we are going.

Often progression needs the assistance of an individual. Many people have been instrumental in a beneficial progression. They have seen a problem, realised it could be fixed and therefore named it 'only worth visiting', and done something about it. One of the best examples of this is Fred Hollows. Fred Hollows was a specialised eye surgeon. But he was more than that, he specialised in taking eye surgery to people who needed it most but could not afford it. Trachoma and cataracts cause blindness in millions of people throughout the third world, despite the fact it can be cured with a very simple surgical procedure. Fred Hollows saw this need and took action. Similar problems could be found in Aboriginal communities in Australia. Hollows set up assistance plans in not only Australia but Eritrea, Nepal, and Vietnam. Now Hollows has passed on—a reminder that no person is forever. But, before he died, he set up a trust fund which ensured that his work continues. 'We are only visiting' can be a comfort, as it almost promises us that we will move beyond even the most horrible of problems. It is a good thing that thanks to individuals like Hollows, we are 'only visiting' such problems.

There have been many scientific advancements made by people. But often the scientists are only there to monitor natural and inevitable progression. Recent scientific discoveries have shown us that genetics are responsible for much of our alterations and evolution as a species. Well, the latest scientific discovery, which will certainly delight some in the room, is that the natural blonde is dying out. Yes, soon dying will be all that's left of our fair-haired friends. The hair-colour stereotype that gentlemen apparently prefer will not occur naturally for very much longer. In fact, the author Kathy Phillips says, 'There's no doubt about it, the blonde is on the brink of extinction ... it is an endangered species.' This shows us that even the simplest things that we take for granted, change. Nothing is static. We are only visiting so we should not only enjoy what we have, while we have it, but also look forward to the next place we are going.

There is one element of this progression of life that is never very enjoyable, and that is the concept of death. No person is forever, and it is a sad but true fact that people die. For this reason, it is important to look out for those around you. To appreciate people while they are there. Now I have done many public speaking competitions, and there are few people who always come—the usual suspects you might say. One such person is my aunty Margaret ... but she's not here tonight. Let me assure you, she is fine ... unfortunately her mother-in-law passed away and so tonight she is at home with her husband, children and grandchildren. Now I often mention family members and friends in my speeches and my  aunty Margaret always says she is waiting for her mention ... well here it is. My aunty is fantastic because she is always there for people. She is always there for me and that is something I really appreciate. You see, we are only visiting, nothing and indeed no person is forever and so we need to appreciate those around us because one day, they may be gone for good.

'We are only visiting' because nothing is forever, nothing but caring for those around you.

Progression may rely on an individual's actions, as seen by Fred Hollows. But this also shows how progression is a good thing and is worth ... well ... how do you put a price on an individual's sight? Progression is also something inevitable, something we can monitor but something no one can escape. Finally, it is important that we care for people, and we make people feel like they belong. Because the world is moving so fast, it can easily leave people behind. And we can't afford to lose anyone. 'We are only visiting' because nothing is forever. Progression is a huge encompassing thing. Something that can easily swallow us up if we are not careful.

I was not the one who upset little Joshua by saying good-bye. The truth is, I never say good-bye. I do this because my grandmother always used to say: 'never say good-bye, because you are always coming back'. And it's true. The world may be constantly progressing, but I think people will always be the most important things to us. We should never forget that and be extra careful to make sure we don't say 'goodbye' to someone for good. 'We are only visiting' so enjoy every moment!